Good Housekeeping

30 MINUTE
COOK BOOK

Good Housekeeping

30 MINUTE COOK BOOK

DELICIOUS DISHES FROM START TO FINISH IN JUST HALF AN HOUR

COLLINS & BROWN

First published in the United Kingdom in 2012 by
Collins & Brown
10 Southcombe Street
London
W14 0RA

An imprint of Anova Books Company Ltd

The Good Housekeeping website is
www.allboutyou.com/goodhousekeeping

10 9 8 7 6 5 4 3 2 1

ISBN 978-1-90844-942-9

A catalogue record for this book is available from the British
Library.

Reproduction by Dot Gradations Ltd, UK
Printed and bound by Craft Print, Singapore

This book can be ordered direct from the publisher at
www.anovabooks.com

PICTURE CREDITS

Photographers: Neil Barclay (pages 15 and 18); Steve Baxter (pages
33, 48, 54, 56, 66, 70, 81, 100, 118, 134, 136, 138, 139, 141, 142, 148, 157, 158,
170, 178, 219, 228, 229, 230, 245, 256, 279, 320 and 327); Martin Brigdale
(pages 152, 187, 202, 252, 294 and 321); Nicki Dowey (pages 10, 11, 12, 14,
16, 17, 20, 22, 25, 26, 43, 53, 90, 103, 106, 107, 114, 149, 166, 181, 191, 200,
204, 212, 225, 232, 234, 242, 260, 265, 266, 268, 270 ,276, 288, 293, 297, 304
and 316); Will Heap (page 207); Fiona Kennedy (page 78); William
Lingwood (pages 30 and 311); Gareth Morgans (pages 34, 35, 37, 40, 44,
50, 60, 65, 67, 68, 87, 88, 93, 94, 98, 101, 122, 124, 126, 127, 128, 131, 132, 133,
146, 155, 162,164, 167, 184, 206, 227, 231, 238, 240, 246, 247, 248, 285, 308,
315 and 319); Myles New (pages 13, 39, 49, 57, 72, 73, 74, 105, 110, 196, 224,
235, 264, 269, 281, 300, 324 and 328); Craig Robertson (pages 21, 23, 63,
169, 188, 195, 209, 211, 213, 222, 223, 236, 237, 254, 271, 273, 275, 290, 296
and 317); Brett Stevens (pages 165 and 177); Lucinda Symons (pages
64, 79, 84, 121, 135, 173, 174, 175, 180, 183, 185, 192, 201, 216, 263, 274, 282
and 289); Phillip Webb (pages 75, 108, 154, 203, 210 and 303); Jon
Whitaker (pages 113, 145, 161, 176, 220 and 259); Kate Whitaker (pages
38, 47, 71, 77, 89, 97, 102, 111, 156, 280, 299, 307, 312 and 323).

Home Economists: Joanna Farrow, Emma Jane Frost, Teresa
Goldfinch, Alice Hart, Lucy McKelvie, Kim Morphew,
Bridget Sargeson and Mari Mererid Williams.

Stylists: Tamzin Ferdinando, Wei Tang, Helen Trent and Fanny Ward.

Contents

Foreword   6

START THE DAY   8

SOUPS AND STARTERS   28

LIGHT BITES AND SIDES   58

SUPER SALADS   82

PASTA DISHES   116

FISH SUPPERS   150

MEAT-FREE MEALS   198

WEEKDAY SUPPERS   214

COOKING FOR FRIENDS   250

PUDDINGS AND SWEET TREATS   286

Index   332

Foreword

I love food that's bursting with flavour – but I know that recipes with long lists of ingredients are immediately off-putting to busy people. After all, who's got time to wade through complicated instructions, then traipse around shops desperately searching for obscure ingredients? And not to mention spending hours slaving over a hot stove...

Don't get me wrong, gourmet meals are great for weekend entertaining, or if you are catering for a special occasion, but what we all really want is practical mid-week eating solutions. You want to feed your family and yourself well but realise time isn't always on your side in the kitchen. This is why this fantastic cookbook will become your saviour – quick, easy and practical meals, with no compromise on flavour.

Each recipe has been triple tested for taste and reliability. The reputation of Good Housekeeping means you can relax as you get cooking as you have a guarantee that the recipes will work and taste wonderful.

Read on and be inspired!

Meike.

Meike Beck
Cookery Editor
Good Housekeeping

Start the Day

Porridge with Dried Fruit

Preparation Time
5 minutes
Cooking Time
5 minutes

- 200g (7oz) porridge oats
- 400ml (14fl oz) milk, plus extra to serve
- 75g (3oz) mixture of chopped dried figs, apricots and raisins

NUTRITIONAL INFORMATION
Per Serving 279 calories,
6g fat (of which 1g saturates),
49g carbohydrate, 0.2g salt

Serves 4

1   Put the oats into a large pan and add the milk and 400ml (14fl oz) water. Stir in the figs, apricots and raisins and heat gently, stirring until the porridge thickens and the oats are cooked.

2   Divide among four bowls and serve with a splash of milk.

Toasted Oats with Berries

Preparation Time
10 minutes, plus cooling
Cooking Time
5-10 minutes

- 25g (1oz) hazelnuts, roughly chopped
- 125g (4oz) rolled oats
- 1 tbsp olive oil
- 125g (4oz) strawberries, sliced
- 250g (9oz) blueberries
- 200g (7oz) Greek yogurt
- 2 tbsp runny honey

NUTRITIONAL
INFORMATION
Per Serving 327 calories,
15g fat (of which 3g saturates),
44g carbohydrate, 0.1g salt

Serves 4

Cook's Tip
Blueberries contain a substance that helps the gut to stay clean and healthy, and, like cranberries, they are rich in antioxidants.

Try Something Different
Use a mixture of raspberries, blackberries, or chopped nectarines or peaches instead of the strawberries and blueberries.

1 Preheat the grill to medium. Put the hazelnuts into a bowl with the oats. Drizzle with the oil and mix well, then spread out on a baking sheet. Toast the oat mixture for 5–10 minutes until it starts to crisp up. Remove from the heat and leave to cool.

2 Put the strawberries into a large bowl with the blueberries and yogurt. Stir in the oats and hazelnuts, drizzle with the honey and divide among four dishes. Serve immediately.

Energy-boosting Muesli

Preparation Time
5 minutes

- 500g (1lb 2oz) porridge oats
- 100g (3½oz) toasted almonds, chopped
- 2 tbsp pumpkin seeds
- 2 tbsp sunflower seeds
- 100g (3½oz) ready-to-eat dried apricots, chopped
- milk or yogurt to serve

NUTRITIONAL INFORMATION
Per Serving 208 calories,
9g fat (of which trace saturates),
28g carbohydrate, 0g salt

Makes 15 servings

Cook's Tip
Oats contain gluten and, strictly speaking, are not suitable for coeliacs. However, because they contain a much smaller amount than wheat, rye or barley, research shows that most people with coeliac disease can safely eat moderate amounts. The oats must be from a source where there is no risk of contamination from wheat or wheat products during processing or packing. As individual tolerance to gluten varies, if you are a coeliac, seek expert advice before eating oats.

1   Mix the oats with the almonds, seeds and apricots. Store in a sealable container: it will keep for up to one month. Serve with milk or yogurt.

Cheesy Spinach Muffins

Preparation Time
15 minutes
Cooking Time
12–15 minutes

- 100g (3½oz) baby spinach
- 150g (5oz) self-raising flour
- 1 tsp baking powder
- 25g (1oz) vegetarian Parmesan-style cheese, grated
- 50g (2oz) vegetarian Cheddar, finely cubed (see Cook's Tip, page 31)
- 25g (1oz) butter, melted
- 100ml (3½fl oz) milk
- 2 medium eggs
- a small handful of fresh parsley, finely chopped
- salt and ground black pepper

NUTRITIONAL INFORMATION
Per Serving 204 calories,
10g fat (6g saturates),
20g carbohydrate, 0.8g salt

Get Ahead
Prepare the muffins to the end of step 2 up to one day in advance. Put the chopped spinach into a bowl, then cover and chill. Cover the flour and cheese mixture and chill, then complete the recipe to serve.

Makes 6 muffins

1 Preheat the oven to 200°C (180°C fan) mark 6. Line six holes in a 12-hole muffin tin with paper cases. Put the spinach into a sieve and pour over boiling water from the kettle until it wilts. Leave the spinach to cool, then squeeze out as much water as you can before finely chopping it. Put to one side.

2 In a large bowl, mix together the flour, baking powder, most of the Parmesan and Cheddar cheeses and some seasoning.

3 In a separate jug, whisk together the butter, milk, eggs, parsley and chopped spinach. Quickly mix the wet ingredients into the dry. Don't worry if there are floury lumps, as these will cook out.

4 Divide the mixture evenly among the paper cases, then sprinkle over the remaining cheeses. Cook for 12–15 minutes until the muffins are risen, golden and cooked through. Serve warm.

Creamy Baked Eggs

Preparation Time
5 minutes
Cooking Time
15–18 minutes

- butter to grease
- 4 sun-dried tomatoes
- 4 medium eggs
- 4 tbsp double cream
- salt and ground black pepper
- Granary bread to serve (optional)

NUTRITIONAL
INFORMATION
Per Serving **153 calories,**
14g fat (of which 7g saturates),
1g carbohydrate, 0.2g salt

Serves 4

1   Preheat the oven to 180°C (160°C fan oven) mark 4. Grease four individual ramekins.

2   Put a tomato into each ramekin and season to taste with salt and pepper. Carefully break an egg on top of each tomato, then drizzle 1 tbsp cream over each egg.

3   Bake for 15–18 minutes – the eggs will continue to cook once they have been taken out of the oven.

4   Leave to stand for 2 minutes before serving. Serve with Granary bread, if you like.

Scrambled Eggs with Smoked Salmon

Preparation Time
10 minutes
Cooking Time
5 minutes

- 6 large eggs
- 25g (1oz) butter, plus extra to spread
- 100g (3½oz) mascarpone cheese
- 125g pack smoked salmon, sliced, or smoked salmon trimmings
- 6 slices sourdough or rye bread, toasted, buttered and cut into slim rectangles for soldiers
- salt and ground black pepper

NUTRITIONAL
INFORMATION
Per Serving 457 calories,
34g fat (of which 17g saturates),
17g carbohydrate, 2.7g salt

Serves 4

1   Crack the eggs into a jug and lightly beat together. Season well.

2   Melt the butter in a non-stick pan over a low heat. Add the eggs and stir constantly until the mixture thickens. Add the mascarpone and season well. Cook for 1–2 minutes longer, until the mixture just becomes firm, then fold in the smoked salmon. Serve at once with toasted bread soldiers.

Beans on Toast

Preparation Time
5 minutes
Cooking Time
10 minutes

- 1 tbsp olive oil
- 2 garlic cloves, finely sliced
- 400g can borlotti or cannellini beans, drained and rinsed
- 400g can chickpeas
- 400g can chopped tomatoes
- leaves from 2 fresh rosemary sprigs, finely chopped
- 4 thick slices Granary bread
- 25g (1oz) Parmesan
- chopped fresh parsley to serve

NUTRITIONAL INFORMATION
Per Serving 364 calories,
9g fat (of which 2g saturates),
55g carbohydrate, 2.1g salt

Serves 4

Try Something Different
This will be just as good with toasted soda bread or seeded bread, mixed beans instead of borlotti or cannellini, and grated Gruyère cheese or Cheddar instead of Parmesan.

1   Heat the oil in a pan over a low heat, add the garlic and cook for 1 minute, stirring gently.

2   Add the beans and chickpeas to the pan with the tomatoes and bring to the boil. Add the rosemary, then reduce the heat and simmer for 8–10 minutes until thickened.

3   Meanwhile, toast the bread and put on to plates. Grate the Parmesan into the bean mixture, stir once, then spoon over the bread. Serve immediately, scattered with parsley.

BLT-topped Bagels with Hollandaise Sauce

Preparation Time
15 minutes
Cooking Time
8 minutes

- 3 large bagels, cut in half horizontally
- 25g (1oz) butter, softened
- 12 smoked streaky bacon rashers, rind removed
- 2 tsp olive oil
- 3 tomatoes, cut into thick slices
- 150ml (¼ pint) bought hollandaise sauce
- 75g (3oz) rocket leaves
- crushed black pepper to garnish

NUTRITIONAL
INFORMATION
Per Serving 384 calories,
31g fat (of which 16g saturates),
16g carbohydrate, 1.9g salt

Serves 6

1   Preheat the grill to high, then grill the halved bagels until golden. Spread generously with the butter. Cover the bagels with a piece of foil and keep them warm. Grill the bacon for 2–3 minutes until crisp, then keep warm. Heat the oil in a small frying pan until very hot and fry the tomatoes for about 1 minute until lightly charred.

2   Put the hollandaise sauce in a small pan and heat gently. To assemble, top the warm bagels with a few rocket leaves, the tomatoes and bacon. Spoon the warm hollandaise sauce over the bacon and garnish with the pepper. Serve at once.

Serves 4

French Toast

Preparation Time
5 minutes
Cooking Time
10 minutes

- 2 medium eggs
- 150ml (¼ pint) semi-skimmed milk
- a generous pinch of freshly grated nutmeg or ground cinnamon
- 4 slices white bread, or fruit bread, crusts removed and each slice cut into four fingers
- 50g (2oz) butter
- vegetable oil for frying
- 1 tbsp golden caster sugar

NUTRITIONAL INFORMATION
Per Finger 259 calories, 20g fat (of which 9g saturates), 15g carbohydrate, 0.7g salt

1 Put the eggs, milk and nutmeg or cinnamon into a shallow dish and beat together.

2 Dip the pieces of bread into the mixture, coating them well.

3 Heat half the butter with 1 tbsp oil in a heavy-based frying pan. When the butter is foaming, fry the egg-coated bread pieces in batches, until golden on both sides, adding more butter and oil as needed. Sprinkle with sugar to serve.

Cook's Tips
Use leftover bread for this tasty breakfast or brunch dish.
For a savoury version, use white bread and omit the spice and sugar; serve with tomato ketchup, or with bacon and maple syrup.

Breakfast Bruschetta

Preparation Time
5 minutes
Cooking Time
5 minutes

- 1 ripe banana, peeled and sliced
- 250g (9oz) blueberries
- 200g (7oz) quark cheese
- 4 slices pumpernickel or wheat-free wholegrain bread
- 1 tbsp runny honey

NUTRITIONAL INFORMATION
Per Serving 145 calories, 1g fat (of which 0g saturates), 30g carbohydrate, 0.4g salt

Serves 4

1   Put the banana into a bowl with the blueberries. Spoon in the quark cheese and mix well.

2   Toast the slices of bread on both sides, then spread with the blueberry mixture. Drizzle with the honey and serve immediately.

Orange Eggy Bread

Preparation Time
10 minutes
Cooking Time
15 minutes

- 2 large eggs
- 150ml (¼ pint) milk
- finely grated zest of 1 orange
- 50g (2oz) butter
- 8 slices raisin bread, halved diagonally
- 1 tbsp caster sugar
- vanilla ice cream and orange segments to serve (optional)

NUTRITIONAL
INFORMATION
Per Serving 358 calories,
13g fat (of which 7g saturates),
54g carbohydrate, 1.2g salt

Serves 4

1 Lightly whisk the eggs, milk and orange zest together in a bowl.

2 Heat the butter in a large frying pan over a medium heat. Dip the slices of raisin bread into the egg mixture, then fry on both sides until golden.

3 Sprinkle the bread with the sugar and serve immediately with ice cream and orange slices, if you like.

Lemon and Blueberry Pancakes

Preparation Time
15 minutes
Cooking Time
10–15 minutes

- 125g (4oz) wholemeal plain flour
- 1 tsp baking powder
- ¼ tsp bicarbonate of soda
- 2 tbsp golden caster sugar
- finely grated zest of 1 lemon
- 125g (4oz) natural yogurt
- 2 tbsp milk
- 2 medium eggs
- 40g (1½oz) butter
- 100g (3½oz) blueberries
- 1 tsp sunflower oil
- natural yogurt and fruit compote to serve

NUTRITIONAL INFORMATION
Per Serving 290 calories,
13g fat (of which 6g saturates),
39g carbohydrate, 0.6g salt

Try Something Different
Instead of blueberries and lemon, use 100g (3½oz) chopped ready-to-eat dried apricots and 2 tsp grated fresh root ginger.

Serves 4

1   Sift the flour, baking powder and bicarbonate of soda into a bowl, tipping in the contents left in the sieve. Add the sugar and lemon zest. Pour in the yogurt and milk. Break the eggs into the mixture and whisk together.

2   Melt 25g (1oz) butter in a pan, add to the bowl with the blueberries and stir everything together.

3   Heat a dot of butter with the oil in a frying pan over a medium heat until hot. Add four large spoonfuls of the mixture to the pan to make four pancakes. After about 2 minutes, flip them over and cook for 1–2 minutes. Repeat with the remaining mixture, adding a dot more butter each time.

4   Serve with natural yogurt and some fruit compote.

Banana and Pecan Muffins

Preparation Time
10 minutes
Cooking Time
20 minutes

- 275g (10oz) self-raising flour
- 1 tbsp bicarbonate of soda
- 1 tsp salt
- 3 very ripe large bananas, about 450g (1lb), peeled and mashed
- 125g (4oz) golden caster sugar
- 1 large egg
- 50ml (2fl oz) milk
- 75g (3oz) melted butter
- 50g (2oz) chopped roasted pecan nuts

NUTRITIONAL
INFORMATION
Per Muffin 236 calories,
9g fat (of which 4g saturates),
37g carbohydrate, 0.8g salt

Makes 12 muffins

Cook's Tip
The secret to really light, fluffy muffins is a light hand, so be sure to sift the flour. Stir the mixture as little as possible; it's okay if it looks a little lumpy. Over-mixing will give tough, chewy results.

1 Preheat the oven to 180°C (160°C fan oven) mark 4. Line a muffin tin with 12 paper cases. Sift together the flour, bicarbonate of soda and salt and put to one side.

2 Combine the bananas, sugar, egg and milk, then pour in the melted butter and mix well. Add to the flour mixture with the nuts, stirring quickly and gently with just a few strokes. Half-fill the muffin cases.

3 Bake for 20 minutes or until golden and risen. Transfer to a wire rack and leave to cool.

Apple Compôte

Preparation Time
10 minutes, plus chilling
Cooking Time
5 minutes

- 250g (9oz) cooking apples, peeled and chopped
- juice of ½ lemon
- 1 tbsp golden caster sugar
- ground cinnamon

TO SERVE
- 25g (1oz) raisins
- 25g (1oz) chopped almonds
- 1 tbsp natural yogurt

NUTRITIONAL
INFORMATION
Per Serving 188 calories,
7g fat (of which 1g saturates),
29g carbohydrate, 0g salt

1   Put the cooking apples into a pan with the lemon juice, caster sugar and 2 tbsp cold water. Cook gently for 5 minutes or until soft. Transfer to a bowl.

2   Sprinkle a little ground cinnamon over the top, cool and chill. It will keep for up to three days.

3   Serve with the raisins, chopped almonds and yogurt.

Cook's Tip
To microwave, put the apples, lemon juice, sugar and water into a microwave-proof bowl, cover loosely with clingfilm and cook on full power in an 850W microwave oven for 4 minutes or until the apples are just soft.

Serves 2

Serves 2
Makes 600ml (1 pint)

Brazil Nut and Banana Smoothie

Preparation Time
10 minutes

- 6 shelled Brazil nuts
- 1 lemon
- 1 small ripe banana
- 1 small ripe avocado
- 1 tsp clear honey
- 400ml (14fl oz) low-fat dairy
  or soya milk, well chilled
- 2 tsp wheatgerm

**NUTRITIONAL
INFORMATION**
Per Serving 310 calories,
19g fat (of which 4g saturates),
25g carbohydrate, 0.3g salt

1   Grind the nuts in a spice grinder or food processor – the mixture needs to be very fine to obtain a good blend.

2   Using a sharp knife, cut off the peel from the lemon, removing as much of the white pith as possible. Chop the flesh roughly, discarding any pips. Peel and roughly chop the banana. Halve the avocado and remove the stone. Peel and roughly chop.

3   Put the nuts, lemon, banana and avocado into a blender with the honey and milk and whiz until smooth. Pour into two glasses and sprinkle with the wheatgerm.

Cook's Tip
This is a lusciously thick, protein-rich drink; add more milk if you like.

Soups and Starters

Serves 6

Parsnip and Stilton Soup

Preparation Time
15 minutes
Cooking Time
about 15 minutes

- 1 medium onion, roughly chopped
- 1 celery stick, roughly chopped
- 9 parsnips, roughly chopped
- 3 tbsp olive oil
- 1.5 litres (2½ pints) vegetable stock
- 100g (3½oz) bread, cut into 1cm (½in) cubes
- 75g (3oz) Stilton
- salt and ground black pepper

NUTRITIONAL
INFORMATION
Per serving 169 calories,
11g fat (of which 4g saturates),
10g carbohydrate, 1.4g salt

1   Whiz the onion, celery and parsnips in a food processor until finely chopped. Heat 2 tbsp of the oil in a large pan and fry the chopped vegetables for 2–3 minutes until beginning to soften. Season well.

2   Pour in the stock and simmer for 10 minutes, stirring occasionally, until the vegetables are tender. Meanwhile, heat the remaining oil in a frying pan over a high heat and fry the bread cubes until golden. Put to one side.

3   Blend the soup in a blender or food processor, in batches if necessary, until smooth. Check the seasoning and divide the soup among six warmed soup bowls. Crumble some Stilton into each bowl, then add croûtons and serve immediately.

Get Ahead
Make the soup and croûtons up to one day in advance. Cover the soup and chill, and store the croûtons in an airtight container. Gently reheat the soup and complete the recipe to serve.

Cook's Tip
Some vegetarians prefer to avoid cheeses that have been produced by the traditional method, because this uses animal-derived rennet. However, most supermarkets and cheese shops now stock an excellent range of vegetarian cheeses, produced using vegetarian rennet. Always check the label when buying.

Spiced Pumpkin Soup

Preparation Time
10 minutes
Cooking Time
20 minutes

- 600g (1lb 5oz) pumpkin flesh, roughly chopped
- 2 celery sticks, roughly chopped
- 1 garlic clove, roughly chopped
- 1 tsp each ground cumin and coriander
- 800ml (1 pint 7fl oz) vegetable stock
- 200ml (7fl oz) coconut milk
- 1 tbsp pumpkin seeds
- salt and ground black pepper
- crusty bread to serve

NUTRITIONAL
INFORMATION
Per serving 222 calories,
20g fat (of which 15g saturates),
8g carbohydrate, 0.8g salt

1   Put the pumpkin flesh into a food processor and whiz for 30 seconds until almost smooth. Add the celery, garlic and spices and whiz again for 30 seconds. Empty into a large pan.

2   Pour over the stock and coconut milk, bring to the boil, then cover, reduce the heat and simmer for 15 minutes.

3   Remove from the heat and blend until smooth (do this in batches, if necessary). Check the seasoning and ladle into warmed soup bowls. Sprinkle with pumpkin seeds and pepper. Serve with crusty bread.

Serves 4

Roasted Red Pepper and Tomato Soup

Preparation Time
10 minutes
Cooking Time
10 minutes

- ½ tbsp extra virgin olive oil, plus extra for drizzling
- 1 red onion, finely chopped
- 2 garlic cloves, roughly chopped
- 6 large tomatoes, roughly chopped
- 200g (7oz) roasted red peppers, roughly chopped
- 600ml (1 pint) hot vegetable stock
- a large handful of fresh basil, roughly chopped
- a little cream for drizzling (optional)
- crusty bread to serve

NUTRITIONAL
INFORMATION
Per serving 67 calories,
3g fat (of which 0.5g saturates),
9g carbohydrate, 1.1g salt

Serves 4

1 Heat the oil in a large pan over a medium heat. Add the onion and cook for 5 minutes until softened. Stir in the garlic and tomatoes and cook for a further 5 minutes.

2 Spoon the tomato mixture into a blender, then add the peppers, stock and most of the basil. Blend in a blender or food processor until smooth, then check the seasoning. Reheat in a pan if necessary. Ladle into warmed soup bowls, then drizzle with the oil and cream (if using). Garnish with the remaining basil and pepper. Serve immediately with crusty bread.

Fast Fish Soup

Preparation Time
10 minutes
Cooking Time
20 minutes

- 1 onion, chopped
- 1 fennel bulb, roughly chopped
- 1 tbsp vegetable oil
- 400g can chopped tomatoes
- 500ml (17fl oz) fish stock
- 1 bay leaf
- finely grated zest of 1 lemon
- 300g (11oz) smoked haddock or smoked cod, diced
- a large handful of chopped fresh parsley
- salt and ground black pepper
- wholemeal bread to serve

NUTRITIONAL
INFORMATION
Per serving **134** calories,
4g fat (of which 1g saturates),
7g carbohydrate, 2g salt

Serves 4

1   Pulse the onion and fennel in a food processor until pea size. Heat the oil in a large pan and fry the chopped vegetables over a medium heat for 10 minutes until soft. Add the tomatoes, stock, bay leaf and lemon zest.

2   Bring to the boil, then add the fish and cook for 2–3 minutes or until the fish is cooked and opaque. Season. Remove the bay leaf and add the parsley. Serve with wholemeal bread.

Creamy Mussel Chowder

Preparation Time
10 minutes
Cooking Time
15 minutes

- 1 tbsp olive oil
- 1 large leek, trimmed and finely chopped
- 2 medium potatoes, finely diced
- 6 smoked streaky bacon rashers, finely chopped
- 250ml (9fl oz) white wine
- 300ml (½ pint) fish stock
- 200ml (7fl oz) double cream
- 198g can sweetcorn, drained
- 800g (1lb 12oz) fresh mussels, cleaned (see Cook's Tip)
- a small handful of each fresh curly parsley and chives, roughly chopped
- salt and ground black pepper
- crusty bread or skinny chips to serve

NUTRITIONAL
INFORMATION
Per serving 588 calories,
42g fat (of which 21g saturates),
32g carbohydrate, 3g salt

1   Heat the oil in a large pan over a medium heat and fry the leek, potatoes and bacon for 5 minutes until the vegetables are nearly tender. Pour over the wine, stock and cream, then cover and bring to the boil. Remove the lid, reduce the heat and simmer for 3 minutes.

2   Add the sweetcorn, mussels and some seasoning. Cover and simmer for 4 minutes or until the mussels are fully open, discard any that remain closed. Stir in the herbs and check the seasoning. Serve immediately with crusty bread to mop up the juices, or better still, some skinny chips.

Cook's Tip
To prepare fresh mussels, rinse them under cold running water to help rid them of any grit and sand. Scrub the mussel shells thoroughly, using a small stiff brush to remove any grit and barnacles. Pull away the hairy 'beard', which protrudes from the one side of the shell. Tap any open mussels sharply with the back of the knife or on the surface. If they refuse to close, throw them away. Rinse the mussels again under cold running water before cooking.

Serves 4

Pea, Parmesan and Chorizo Soup

Preparation Time
15 minutes
Cooking Time
about 10 minutes, plus cooling

- 1 tbsp olive oil
- 1 large onion, roughly chopped
- 40g (1½oz) Parmesan, grated
- 75g (3oz) chorizo, skinned and finely cubed
- 750g (1lb 11oz) frozen peas
- 1.2 litres (2¼ pints) hot vegetable stock
- salt and ground black pepper

NUTRITIONAL INFORMATION
Per serving 180 calories,
9g fat (of which 3g saturates),
14g carbohydrate, 1.3g salt

Get Ahead
Complete the recipe to the end of step 3 up to 2 hours in advance. Chill the soup and store the Parmesan and chorizo (in its pan) at a cool room temperature. To serve, gently reheat the chorizo in the pan before completing the recipe to serve.

Serves 6

1 Preheat the oven to 220°C (200°C fan) mark 7. Heat the oil in a large pan and gently fry the onion for 5 minutes.

2 Meanwhile, sprinkle the Parmesan over a small non-stick baking sheet and cook in the oven for 5 minutes until golden and bubbling. Fry the chorizo in a small frying pan for 2–3 minutes until some of the oil has leaked out. Set aside. Take the Parmesan out of the oven, leave to harden slightly, then use a spatula to lift the cheese off the baking sheet. Put on to a wire rack to cool.

3 Add the peas and stock to the onion pan and bring to the boil. Take off the heat and blend in a blender or food processor until smooth. Return to the pan and check the seasoning.

4 To serve, reheat the soup if necessary, then divide among six warmed soup bowls. Break the Parmesan into shards. Garnish the soups with the Parmesan shards, chorizo and chorizo oil. Serve immediately.

Sweetcorn and Bacon Chowder

Preparation Time
10 minutes
Cooking Time
20 minutes

- 1 tbsp olive oil
- 200g (7oz) smoked bacon lardons
- 1 large onion, finely chopped
- 2 celery sticks, chopped
- 2 large carrots, chopped
- ¼ tsp each ground cinnamon and smoked paprika
- 1.3 litres (2¼ pints) vegetable stock
- 2 × 198g cans sweetcorn, drained
- 250ml (8fl oz) double cream
- a large handful of fresh parsley, roughly chopped
- salt and ground black pepper
- breadsticks to serve

NUTRITIONAL
INFORMATION
Per serving 406 calories,
33g fat (of which 17g saturates),
21g carbohydrate, 2.3g salt

Get Ahead
Complete the recipe up to one
day in advance, omitting the
parsley. Leave to cool, empty
into a bowl, then cover and chill.
To serve, reheat in a pan and
complete the recipe.

Serves 6

1   Heat the oil in a large pan and fry the lardons, chopped vegetables and spices for 5–10 minutes until the vegetables are soft.

2   Pour in the stock, bring to the boil, then reduce the heat and simmer for 5 minutes or until the vegetables are tender. Add the sweetcorn, cream, and most of the parsley and simmer for a further 2–3 minutes. Check the seasoning and divide the soup among six warmed mugs or bowls. Garnish with the remaining parsley and serve with breadsticks.

Serves 4

Hot and Sour Pork Soup

Preparation Time
10 minutes
Cooking Time
about 10 minutes

- 1 tbsp oil
- 450g (1lb) pork fillet, cut into strips
- 2 peppers, seeded and cut into thin strips
- 1 red chilli, sliced into rings
- 1 carrot, cut into thin strips
- juice of 1 lime
- 2 tbsp palm or brown sugar
- 1 tbsp miso paste
- 1 tsp fish sauce
- 2 spring onions, thinly sliced
- 150g (5oz) bean sprouts
- salt and ground black pepper

NUTRITIONAL
INFORMATION
Per serving 272 calories,
11g fat (of which 3g saturates),
17g carbohydrate, 0.9g salt

1 Heat the oil in a pan over a high heat and fry the pork and peppers for about 5 minutes until golden.

2 Add the chilli, carrot, lime juice, sugar, miso paste, fish sauce and 1 litre (1¾ pints) boiling water and simmer for 5 minutes. Stir through the spring onions and bean sprouts, then check the seasoning and serve.

Herb and Lemon Soup

Preparation Time
10 minutes
Cooking Time
15 minutes

- 1.7 litres (3 pints) chicken stock
- 150g (5oz) orzo or other dried soup pasta
- 3 medium eggs
- juice of 1 large lemon
- 2 tbsp finely chopped fresh chives
- 2 tbsp finely chopped fresh chervil
- salt and ground black pepper
- lemon wedges to serve

NUTRITIONAL INFORMATION
Per serving 130 calories,
4g fat (of which 1g saturates),
18g carbohydrate, 1.8g salt

1   Bring the stock to the boil in a large pan. Add the pasta and cook for 5 minutes or according to the pack instructions.

2   Beat the eggs in a bowl until frothy, then add the lemon juice and 1 tbsp cold water. Slowly stir in two ladlefuls of the hot stock. Put the egg mixture into the pan with the rest of the stock, then warm through over a very low heat for 2–3 minutes

3   Add the chives and chervil and season with salt and pepper. Ladle the soup into warmed bowls and serve immediately, with lemon wedges.

Serves 6

Serves 4

Pork and Miso Noodle Soup

Preparation Time
15 minutes
Cooking Time
15 minutes

- 1 tbsp vegetable oil
- 400g (14oz) pork fillet, cut into finger-size strips
- 100g (3½oz) mangetouts, halved
- 4cm (1½in) piece fresh root ginger, peeled and finely grated
- 1 orange pepper, seeded and finely sliced
- 1 tbsp miso paste
- 150g (5oz) rice or egg noodles
- a few drops Tabasco sauce
- salt and ground black pepper
- 3 spring onions, finely sliced and a large handful of fresh coriander, roughly chopped, to garnish

NUTRITIONAL
INFORMATION
Per serving 358 calories,
11g fat (of which 3g saturates),
36g carbohydrate, 0.5g salt

1   Heat the oil in a large pan or wok over a high heat. Add the pork and cook for 5 minutes, stirring, until golden. Add the mangetouts, ginger and pepper and cook for 3 minutes or until vegetables are soft.

2   Stir in the miso, noodles and 1 litre (1¾ pints) water. Bring to the boil, then reduce the heat and simmer for 2 minutes. Add the Tabasco, check the seasoning, then divide the soup among four bowls. Garnish with spring onions and coriander and serve immediately.

Vietnamese Turkey Noodle Soup

Preparation Time
15 minutes
Cooking Time
about 10 minutes

- 1.8–2 litres (3¼–3½ pints) chicken stock
- 4cm (1½in) piece fresh root ginger, peeled and finely chopped
- 1 garlic clove, finely chopped
- 450g (1lb) turkey breast fillet, sliced into thin strips
- 1 tbsp fish sauce
- ¼ head Savoy cabbage, finely shredded
- 100g (3½oz) rice noodles
- a large handful of bean sprouts
- juice of 1 lime
- 1 large red chilli, seeded and thinly sliced (see Cook's Tips)
- 4 spring onions, sliced
- a large handful each of fresh coriander and mint, roughly chopped, to garnish

NUTRITIONAL INFORMATION
Per serving 288 calories,
2g fat (of which 1g saturates),
24g carbohydrate, 1.7g salt

1 Bring the stock to the boil in a large pan. Add the ginger, garlic and turkey and simmer for 5 minutes.

2 Stir in the fish sauce, cabbage and noodles and cook for 3 minutes (check that the turkey is cooked). Add the bean sprouts, lime juice and most of the chilli and spring onions. Check the seasoning. Divide the soup among four bowls, garnish with the herbs and the remaining chilli and spring onions. Serve immediately.

Cook's Tips
Chillies vary enormously in strength, from quite mild to blisteringly hot, depending on the type of chilli and its ripeness. Taste a small piece first to check it's not too hot for you.
Be extremely careful when handling chillies not to touch or rub your eyes with your fingers, or they will sting. Wash knives immediately after handling chillies. As a precaution, use rubber gloves when preparing them, if you like.

Serves 4

Chunky Pea and Tortelloni Soup

Preparation Time
10 minutes
Cooking Time
about 10 minutes

- 1.2 litres (2¼ pints) vegetable stock
- 250g pack tortelloni, such as spinach and ricotta
- 4 spring onions, roughly chopped
- 750g (1lb 11oz) peas
- 50g (2oz) watercress, plus extra to garnish
- extra virgin olive oil, to drizzle

NUTRITIONAL INFORMATION
Per serving 296 calories,
7g fat (of which 3g saturates),
41g carbohydrate, 1.7g salt

Serves 4

1   Put a sieve over a large jug. Pour the stock into a large pan and bring to the boil. Add the pasta and cook for 3 minutes. Drain into the jug. Put the stock back into the pan and set aside the pasta.

2   Add the spring onions and peas to the stock and simmer for 5 minutes. Add the watercress, then blend in a blender or food processor, in batches if you like, until combined but with a chunky texture. Return to the pan, check the seasoning and reheat if necessary.

3   Divide the soup among four bowls. Top each with a quarter of the tortelloni, a drizzle of oil and a few watercres sprigs.

Healing Chicken and Ginger Broth

Preparation Time
15 minutes
Cooking Time
about 10 minutes

Serves 4

- 3 × 125g (4oz) skinless chicken breasts, cut into strips
- 1.4 litres (2½ pints) strong chicken stock
- 4cm (1½in) piece fresh root ginger, peeled and cut into matchsticks
- ½–1 red chilli, seeded and finely sliced (see Cook's Tips, page 46)
- 125g pack baby sweetcorn, roughly chopped
- 2 large carrots, cut into matchsticks
- 200g (7oz) uncooked egg noodles or 250g (8oz) cooked rice
- 4 spring onions, finely sliced
- a small handful of fresh parsley, finely chopped

NUTRITIONAL INFORMATION
Per serving 370 calories, 8g fat (of which 2g saturates), 41g carbohydrate, 1.8g salt

Cook's Tip
If you have any leftover roast chicken, use this instead of poaching the chicken specially for this soup. Simply add to the simmering stock to warm through for a quick and economical supper.

1 Put the chicken in a medium pan and cover with cold water. Bring to the boil, reduce the heat and simmer gently for 5 minutes or until cooked through.

2 Meanwhile, in a large pan, bring the stock to the boil and add the ginger and chilli. Leave to simmer for a few minutes, then add the sweetcorn, carrots, noodles or rice and most of the spring onions. Simmer for 3 minutes until the noodles, if using, are cooked and the vegetables are just softening.

3 Drain the cooked chicken and divide the broth among four soup bowls. Ladle over the stock mixture, sprinkle over the remaining spring onions and the parsley and serve.

Serves 4

Pea and Ham Soup

Preparation Time
10 minutes
Cooking Time
20 minutes

- 1 tbsp oil
- 1 onion, chopped
- 750g (1lb 11oz) frozen peas
- 1 litre (1¾ pints) chicken stock
- 2 × 200g (7oz) unsmoked gammon steaks, fat trimmed
- 1 tbsp chopped fresh chives, plus extra to garnish
- salt and ground black pepper
- 4 tsp half-fat crème fraîche to garnish
- crusty bread to serve

NUTRITIONAL
INFORMATION
Per serving 378 calories,
21g fat (of which 8g saturates),
21g carbohydrate, 2.9g salt

1   Heat the oil in a large pan, add the onion and fry for 10 minutes until softened but not coloured.

2   Stir in the peas and chicken stock and bring to the boil. Add the gammon steaks, then reduce the heat and simmer for 5 minutes until cooked through.

3   Lift the gammon out and set aside on a board. Blend the soup in a blender or food processor, in batches, if necessary, until completely smooth. Meanwhile, shred the gammon into fine pieces, discarding any fat.

4   Return the soup to the pan, reheat, then add the shredded gammon and chives. Check the seasoning. Divide the soup among four warmed soup bowls and garnish with some crème fraîche, extra chives and pepper. Serve with crusty bread.

Broccoli and Goat's Cheese Soup

Preparation Time
10 minutes
Cooking Time
20 minutes

- 50g (2oz) butter
- 2 medium onions, chopped
- 1 litre (1¾ pints) vegetable, chicken or turkey stock
- 700g (1½lb) broccoli, broken into florets, stout stalks peeled and chopped
- 1 head of garlic, separated into cloves, unpeeled
- 1 tbsp olive oil
- 150g (5oz) goat's cheese
- salt and ground black pepper

NUTRITIONAL
INFORMATION
Per Serving **220 calories,**
16g fat (of which 10g saturates),
8g carbohydrate, 0.5g salt

1   Preheat the oven to 200°C (180°C fan oven) mark 6. Melt the butter in a pan over a gentle heat. Add the onions, then cover the pan and cook for 4–5 minutes until translucent. Add half the stock and bring to the boil. Add the broccoli and bring back to the boil, then cover the pan, reduce the heat and simmer for 15–20 minutes until the broccoli is tender.

2   Meanwhile, toss the cloves of garlic in the oil and tip into a roasting tin. Roast in the oven for 15 minutes or until soft when squeezed.

3   Leave the soup to cool a little, then add the goat's cheese and whiz in batches in a blender or food processor until smooth. Return the soup to the pan and add the remaining stock. Reheat gently on the hob and season to taste with salt and pepper.

4   Ladle the soup into warmed bowls, squeeze the garlic out of their skins and scatter over the soup, add a sprinkling of black pepper and serve.

Try Something Different
Double the quantity of goat's cheese, if you prefer a stronger taste. Instead of goat's cheese, substitute a soft garlic cheese for a really garlicky flavour.

Serves 6

Serves 4

Smoky Prawn Cocktail

Preparation Time
5 minutes
Cooking Time
about 5 minutes, plus cooling

- 1 tbsp olive oil
- 1½ tsp smoked paprika
- 600g (1lb 5oz) raw king prawns, peeled (see Cook's Tip)
- 4 tbsp good-quality mayonnaise
- 3 avocados, stoned and sliced
- 200g (7oz) mixed salad leaves
- salt and ground black pepper
- crusty bread to serve (optional)

NUTRITIONAL INFORMATION
Per serving 461 calories, 36g fat (of which 7g saturates), 3g carbohydrate, 1.5g salt

1   Heat the oil in a frying pan, add the smoked paprika and fry for 30 seconds. Add the prawns and cook for a further 2–3 minutes, turning occasionally until they are pink and cooked through. Tip into a bowl and leave to cool completely.

2   Stir the mayonnaise into the prawns and check the seasoning. Divide the sliced avocados, salad leaves and the prawn mixture equally among four glasses or plates and serve with crusty bread, if you like.

Cook's Tip
To devein prawns, pull off the head and discard (or put to one side and use later for making stock). Using pointed scissors, cut through the soft shell on the belly side. Prise off the shell, leaving the tail attached. (The shell can also be used later for making stock.) Using a small sharp knife, make a shallow cut along the back of the prawn. Using the point of the knife, remove and discard the black vein (the intestinal tract) that runs along the back of the prawn.

Halloumi and Pepper Bruschetta

Preparation Time
10 minutes
Cooking Time
15–18 minutes

- 4 large peppers, seeded and sliced
- 2 tbsp extra virgin olive oil
- 250g pack halloumi, thinly sliced
- 8 slices sourdough
- 1 tbsp balsamic vinegar
- a small handful of fresh mint, roughly chopped
- salt and ground black pepper
- tzatziki or houmous and a green salad to serve

NUTRITIONAL INFORMATION
Per serving 491 calories, 24g fat (of which 11g saturates), 46g carbohydrate, 2.7g salt

Serves 4

1 Preheat the grill to medium. Put the pepper slices on a baking sheet, drizzle over half the oil and season well. Grill for 10–12 minutes, tossing occasionally, until the peppers are tender and beginning to colour. Lay the halloumi slices over the peppers and grill for a further 5–6 minutes, turning once, until the cheese is golden.

2 When the cheese is nearly ready, toast the bread. Stir the remaining oil and balsamic vinegar with plenty of seasoning together in a small bowl. Divide the toasts and pepper mixture among four plates, then drizzle over the dressing. Scatter over the mint and season with pepper. Serve immediately with a dollop of tzatziki or houmous and a green salad.

Duck Egg and Asparagus Dippers

Preparation Time
15 minutes
Cooking Time
about 6 minutes

- 600g (1lb 5oz) asparagus spears (not the fine variety)
- 6 duck eggs
- extra virgin olive oil, to drizzle
- salt and cracked black pepper
- sourdough bread (optional) to serve

NUTRITIONAL INFORMATION
Per serving 174 calories, 12g fat (of which 3g saturates), 2g carbohydrate, 0.2g salt

Get Ahead
Prepare the asparagus to the end of step 2 up to 2 hours in advance. Chill the bundles, then complete the recipe to serve.

Serves 6

1   Holding both ends of an asparagus spear in your hands, bend gently until it snaps. Discard the woody end (or keep to make soups or stocks). Trim all the remaining spears to this length. Use a vegetable peeler to shave any knobbly or woody bits below the tip of each spear.

2   Divide the asparagus equally into six piles, then tie each neatly into a bundle with string.

3   Bring two medium pans of water to the boil. Add the eggs to one pan and simmer for exactly 5½ minutes. Add the asparagus bundles to the other pan and cook for 1 minute until just tender. Drain the asparagus and leave to steam-dry in the colander for 3 minutes. Drain the eggs.

4   Put one asparagus bundle on each plate, drizzle with a little extra virgin olive oil and season with salt and pepper. Serve with the eggs, plus a slice of sourdough bread, if you like.

Light Bites and Sides

Serves 4

Pesto Pasta with a Difference

Preparation Time
10 minutes
Cooking Time
10–12 minutes

- 50ml (2fl oz) extra virgin olive oil
- ½ garlic clove, finely chopped
- grated zest and juice of ½ lemon
- 40g (1½oz) grated Parmesan, plus extra to garnish
- 40g (1½oz) pinenuts, toasted
- a large handful of basil, finely chopped, plus extra leaves to garnish
- salt and ground black pepper
- 400g (14oz) dried tagliatelle to serve

NUTRITIONAL INFORMATION
Per serving 579 calories, 25g fat (of which 5g saturates), 75g carbohydrate, 0.2g salt

1   Mix the oil, 50ml (2 fl oz) water, the garlic, lemon zest and juice, grated Parmesan, toasted pinenuts and the chopped basil together in a bowl.

2   Check the seasoning and stir into hot cooked pasta. Garnish with basil leaves and extra grated Parmesan and serve.

Roasted Vegetable Tartlets

Preparation Time
15 minutes
Cooking Time
about 7 minutes

- 375g pack ready-rolled puff pastry, thawed if frozen
- plain flour to dust
- 1 medium egg, beaten
- 2 tbsp coarse sea salt
- 300g (11oz) vegetable antipasti in olive oil
- olive oil, if needed
- 2 tbsp balsamic vinegar
- 190g tub red pepper hummus
- 50g (2oz) wild rocket
- salt and ground black pepper

NUTRITIONAL INFORMATION
Per Tartlet 356 calories,
24g fat (of which 1g saturates),
30g carbohydrate, 1.1g salt

1 Preheat the oven to 220°C (200°C fan oven) mark 7. Unroll the puff pastry on a lightly floured surface and cut it into six squares. Put the pastry squares on a large baking sheet and prick each one all over with a fork. Brush the surface with beaten egg and sprinkle the edges with sea salt. Bake for 5–7 minutes until the pastry is golden brown and cooked through. Press down the centre of each tartlet slightly with the back of a fish slice.

2 Make the dressing. Pour 4 tbsp oil from the jar of antipasti into a bowl (top it up with a little more olive oil if there's not enough in the antipasti jar). Add the vinegar, season with salt and pepper and mix well, then put to one side.

3 To serve, spread some hummus over the central part of each tartlet. Put the tartlets on individual plates and spoon on the antipasti – there's no need to be neat. Whisk the balsamic vinegar dressing. Add the rocket leaves and toss to coat, then pile a small handful of leaves on top of each tartlet. Serve immediately.

Get Ahead
Complete the recipe to the end of step 1. Leave the tartlets to cool on a wire rack, then store in an airtight container. It will keep for up to two days. Complete the recipe to serve.

Makes 6

Couscous-stuffed Mushrooms

Preparation Time
3 minutes
Cooking Time
about 12 minutes

- 125g (4oz) couscous
- 20g pack fresh flat-leafed parsley, roughly chopped
- 280g jar mixed antipasti in oil, drained and oil put to one side
- 8 large flat portabellini mushrooms
- 25g (1oz) butter
- 25g (1oz) plain flour
- 300ml (½ pint) skimmed milk
- 75g (3oz) mature vegetarian Cheddar, grated, plus extra to sprinkle (see Cook's Tip, page 31)
- green salad to serve

NUTRITIONAL
INFORMATION
Per Serving 373 calories,
25g fat (of which 10g saturates),
25g carbohydrate, 0.6g salt

Serves 4

1   Preheat the oven to 220°C (200°C fan oven) mark 7. Put the couscous into a bowl with 200ml (7fl oz) boiling water, the parsley, antipasti and 1 tbsp of the reserved oil. Stir well.

2   Put the mushrooms on a non-stick baking sheet and spoon a little of the couscous mixture into the centre of each. Cook in the oven while you make the sauce.

3   Whisk together the butter, flour and milk in a small pan over a high heat until the mixture comes to the boil. Reduce the heat as soon as it starts to thicken, then whisk constantly until smooth. Take the pan off the heat and stir in the cheese.

4   Spoon the sauce over the mushrooms and sprinkle with the remaining cheese. Put back into the oven for a further 7–10 minutes until golden. Serve with a green salad.

Prawn and Pineapple Skewers

Preparation Time
15 minutes
Cooking Time
about 10 minutes

- 12 wooden skewers
- 300g (11oz) raw peeled king prawns (see Cook's Tip, page 55)
- 400g (14oz) fresh pineapple chunks
- 2 red peppers, seeded and cut into 4cm (1½in) chunks
- ½ tbsp vegetable oil
- grated zest and juice of 2 limes, plus extra wedges to serve
- 1 tsp fish sauce
- 1 tbsp clear honey
- 2cm (¾in) piece fresh root ginger, grated
- 1 garlic clove, finely chopped
- ½–1 red chilli, to taste, seeded and finely chopped (see Cook's Tip, page 46)
- ground black pepper

NUTRITIONAL
INFORMATION
Per serving (three skewers)
153 calories, 2g fat (of which 0.3g saturates), 19g carbohydrate, 0.8g salt

Serves 4

1 Soak the wooden skewers in hot water for 5 minutes. Preheat the grill to medium. Divide the prawns, pineapple and peppers among the presoaked skewers. Arrange the skewers on a baking sheet, brush with oil and grill for 3 minutes on each side, or until the prawns have turned pink and the pineapple and peppers have just started to colour.

2 Stir the remaining ingredients (except the pepper) together in a small bowl then brush a little of the sauce over the cooked skewers. Season the skewers with pepper, then serve with rice, lime wedges and the remaining sauce as a dip.

Chicory with Ham and Cheese

Preparation Time
5 minutes
Cooking Time
about 10 minutes

- 4 large green chicory heads
- 8 slices honey roast ham
- 8 slices Gouda cheese
- 15g (½oz) fresh brown
  breadcrumbs
- crusty bread and a green
  salad to serve

NUTRITIONAL
INFORMATION
Per serving **261 calories, 16g fat
(of which 10g saturates),
9g carbohydrate, 2.3g salt**

Serves 4

1   Bring a large pan of water to the boil. Cut the chicory heads in half
lengthways and simmer for 3–5 minutes until just tender. Drain well.

2   Preheat the grill to medium. Wrap each cooked chicory half in a slice of
ham and arrange, cut side down, on a baking sheet. Lay a piece of cheese
over each chicory half and top with some of the breadcrumbs. Grill for
3–5 minutes until piping hot and golden. Serve with crusty bread and a
green salad.

Chicken Club Sandwich

Preparation Time
20 minutes

- 12 slices good-quality white bread, freshly toasted
- 4 tsp wholegrain mustard
- 3 tomatoes, thinly sliced
- 40g (1½oz) mature Cheddar, grated
- a large handful of fresh basil leaves
- 4 tsp mayonnaise
- 2 cooked skinless chicken breasts, sliced, about 200g (7oz)
- 1 large avocado, stoned and thinly sliced
- a large handful of rocket
- salt and ground black pepper

NUTRITIONAL INFORMATION
Per serving 583 calories, 29g fat (of which 7g saturates), 54g carbohydrate, 1.8g salt

Serves 4

1   Lay four slices of toasted bread on a board. Spread each with 1 tsp mustard, then divide the tomato slices, cheese and basil equally among the four slices. Press another slice of toast on to each stack.

2   Spread the top toast of each stack with 1 tsp mayonnaise, then divide the chicken, avocado and rocket equally among the stacks. Season, then press the final slice of toast on to each stack.

3   Cut the stacks into quarters diagonally, then secure each quarter with a cocktail stick. Serve immediately.

Serves 4

Pizza Bread

Preparation Time
10 minutes
Cooking Time
10 minutes

- 2 × 125g (4oz) part-baked baguettes
- 6 tbsp tomato passata
- ½ red onion, finely sliced
- 125g (4oz) marinated artichoke pieces
- 40g (1½oz) black olives, pitted
- 125g (4oz) ball mozzarella, thinly sliced
- 75g (3oz) cherry tomatoes
- 2 tbsp fresh pesto
- ground black pepper
- crisp green salad to serve

NUTRITIONAL INFORMATION
Per serving 313 calories,
12g fat (of which 5g saturates),
39g carbohydrate, 2.2g salt

1 Preheat the oven to 220°C (200°C fan) mark 7. Slice each baguette in half horizontally and put on a baking sheet, cut side up.

2 Spread 1½ tbsp passata on top of each baguette half then cover the baguettes with the remaining ingredients, dividing the toppings equally among the four halves. Season with pepper. Cook for 10 minutes until the bread is crisp and golden then serve with a crisp green salad.

Welsh Rarebit

Preparation Time
15 minutes
Cooking Time
about 15 minutes

- 400g can chopped tomatoes
- ½ tbsp tomato purée
- 1 small shallot, finely sliced
- 175g (6oz) Caerphilly or mature Cheddar, grated
- ½ tsp English mustard
- 50ml (2fl oz) ale
- Few dashes Worcestershire sauce
- 1 large egg yolk
- 1½ tbsp finely chopped fresh parsley
- 8 crumpets
- salt and ground black pepper
- crisp green salad to serve

NUTRITIONAL INFORMATION
Per serving 389 calories, 18g fat (of which 10g saturates), 41g carbohydrate, 2.8g salt

Serves 4

1 Put the canned tomatoes, tomato purée and shallot into a small pan. Bring to the boil, then reduce the heat and simmer for 10 minutes. Check the seasoning.

2 Meanwhile, mix the cheese, mustard, ale, Worcestershire sauce, egg yolk, parsley and some seasoning together in a bowl.

3 Preheat the grill to medium. Arrange the crumpets on a baking sheet and toast until golden. Divide and spread the tomato sauce equally over the toasted crumpets, then top each with an equal amount of the cheese mixture. Grill for 3–5 minutes until bubbling and golden. Serve with a crisp green salad.

Thyme Tomatoes

Preparation Time
3 minutes
Cooking Time
10–12 minutes

- 500g (1lb 2oz) cherry tomatoes, on the vine
- 1 tbsp olive oil
- 3 fresh thyme sprigs
- salt and ground black pepper

NUTRITIONAL
INFORMATION
Per serving 36 calories,
3g fat (of which 0.5g saturates),
3g carbohydrate, 0g salt

Serves 6

Get Ahead
Complete the recipe to the end of step 1 up to 3 hours in advance. Cover and store at a cool room temperature, then complete the recipe to serve.

1 Preheat the oven to 220°C (200°C fan) mark 7. Trim the tomatoes into small bunches and put the bunches into a small roasting tin. Drizzle over the oil and add the thyme. Season well with salt and pepper.

2 Roast for 10–12 minutes until the tomatoes have burst but are still holding their shape. Remove the thyme and serve immediately.

Poppadom Scoops

Preparation Time
10 minutes

- ¼ red onion, finely chopped
- 1 ripe mango, finely diced
- ½ green chilli, seeded and finely chopped (see Cook's Tips, page 46)
- a small handful of fresh coriander, finely chopped
- grated zest and juice of 1 lime
- 20 mini poppadoms
- salt and ground black pepper

NUTRITIONAL
INFORMATION
Per serving **8 calories**,
0g fat (of which 0g saturates),
2g carbohydrate, 0.1g salt

Makes 20

GET AHEAD
Complete the recipe up the end of step 1 one day in advance, but don't add the coriander. Cover and chill in the fridge, then complete the recipe up to 1 hour before serving.

1   Mix the onion, mango, chilli, coriander, lime zest and juice and some seasoning together in a medium bowl.

2   Spoon into poppadoms and serve.

Spicy Nuts

Preparation Time
10 minutes
Cooking Time
about 20 minutes, plus cooling

- ◆ 450g (1lb) mixed unsalted nuts and seeds, such as hazelnuts, peanuts, cashews, macadamias, Brazil nuts, pumpkin and sunflower seeds
- ◆ 2 tbsp olive oil
- ◆ 1–2 red chillies, seeded and finely chopped (see Cook's Tips, page 46)
- ◆ 1½ tbsp fresh thyme leaves
- ◆ 2 garlic cloves, finely chopped
- ◆ 1¼ tsp rock salt
- ◆ ground black pepper

NUTRITIONAL INFORMATION
Per 25g (1oz) serving
147 calories, 13g fat (of which 2g saturates), 3g carbohydrate, 0g salt

Makes 450g (1lb)

Get Ahead
Complete the recipe up to a week in advance. Cool, then transfer to an airtight container and store at room temperature.

1 Preheat the oven to 200°C (180°C fan) mark 6. Mix together all the ingredients in a large bowl with the rock salt and lots of pepper.

2 Put the nut mixture on to a baking sheet and roast for 15–20 minutes, tossing occasionally, until the nuts are golden. Leave to cool completely, then empty into bowls and serve.

Party Prawns

Preparation Time
10 minutes
Cooking Time
about 5 minutes

- 5–7 rashers streaky bacon
- 150g pack raw king prawns
- 25g (1oz) butter
- 1 tbsp chopped fresh chives
- ground black pepper

NUTRITIONAL INFORMATION
Per serving **38 calories**,
3g fat (of which 1.5g saturates),
0g carbohydrate, 0.2g salt

Makes about 25

Get Ahead
Complete the recipe to the end of step 1 up to 4 hours in advance. Cover and keep in the fridge, then complete the recipe to serve.

1 Slice each bacon rasher in half lengthways, then in half widthways. Wrap a bacon strip around the middle of each raw prawn.

2 Heat the butter in a large frying pan. Add the prawns and cook for 3–5 minutes until the prawns are bright pink and bacon is cooked.

3 Season well with pepper and sprinkle over the chives. Serve immediately with cocktail sticks.

Jumbo Salmon Blini

Preparation Time
20 minutes
Cooking Time
about 10 minutes, plus cooling

- 300ml (½ pint) crème fraîche
- grated zest and juice of ½ lemon, plus lemon wedges to serve (optional)
- 175g (6oz) plain flour
- 1 tsp baking powder
- 3 large eggs, separated
- 200ml (7fl oz) milk
- 3 tbsp chopped fresh chives, plus extra to garnish
- ½ tbsp olive oil
- 210g pack smoked salmon slices
- salt and ground black pepper
- 1 tbsp lumpfish caviar to garnish (optional)

NUTRITIONAL INFORMATION
Per serving 306 calories, 20g fat (of which 11g saturates), 19g carbohydrate, 1.6g salt

Get Ahead
Complete the recipe to the end of step 4 up to 2 hours in advance. Cover and chill the crème fraîche mixture. Cover and keep the blini at cool room temperature. Complete the recipe to serve.

Serves 8

1 Mix the crème fraîche, lemon zest and juice, and salt and pepper to taste together in a small bowl. Put to one side.

2 Sift the flour, baking powder and a pinch of salt into a large bowl. Make a well in the centre and add the egg yolks and milk. Gradually whisk the flour into the liquid to make a smooth batter.

3 In a separate bowl, whisk the egg whites until they form stiff peaks. Use a large metal spoon to fold the egg whites into the batter, then add the chives and some pepper.

4 Preheat the grill to medium. Heat the oil in a 25.5cm (10in) non-stick frying pan. Add the batter and cook over a low-medium heat for 3–4 minutes until the base is golden. Next, grill for 3 minutes until golden and cooked through. Leave the blini to cool for 30 minutes.

5 To serve, put the blini on to a cake stand or serving plate and spoon over the crème fraîche mixture. Top with smoked salmon slices and garnish with extra chives, pepper and lumpfish caviar (if using). Serve with lemon wedges, if you like.

Cajun Fish Wraps

Preparation Time
15 minutes
Cooking Time
3–5 minutes

- grated zest and juice of ½ lime
- 4 tbsp plain yogurt
- 1 tbsp chopped fresh chives
- 25g (1oz) dry polenta
- 1 tbsp Cajun spice
- 375g (13oz) white fish fillets, such as plaice, cod or pollock, cut into finger-size strips
- oil to brush
- 50g (2oz) rocket leaves
- 1 avocado, cut into strips
- 1 red pepper, seeded and cut into strips
- 4 flour tortillas
- salt and ground black pepper
- dressed green salad to serve

NUTRITIONAL
INFORMATION
Per serving 358 calories,
12g fat (of which 2g saturates),
40g carbohydrate, 0.8g salt

1   Mix the lime zest and juice, yogurt, chives and some seasoning together in a small bowl. Put to one side.

2   Preheat the grill to high. Mix the polenta, Cajun spice and a little seasoning together in a medium bowl. Add the fish and coat in the polenta mixture. Brush a baking sheet with some oil and arrange the coated fish on the sheet. Grill for 3–5 minutes until cooked through.

3   Divide the fish, rocket, avocado and pepper equally into four, putting the ingredients in one quarter of each tortilla. Drizzle over the yogurt dressing, then fold each tortilla into quarters to make a pocket. Serve immediately with a dressed green salad.

Serves 4

Carrots with Mint and Lemon

Preparation Time
15 minutes
Cooking Time
15 minutes

Serves 4

- 700g (1½lb) small new carrots, trimmed and scrubbed
- finely grated zest and juice of ½ lemon
- 1 tsp light soft brown sugar
- 15g (½oz) butter
- 2 tbsp freshly chopped mint
- salt and ground black pepper

NUTRITIONAL INFORMATION
Per serving **86 calories**, 4g fat (of which 2g saturates), 12g carbohydrate, 0.5g salt

1   Cook the carrots in lightly salted boiling water for about 10 minutes or until just tender. Drain.

2   Return the carrots to the pan with the remaining ingredients and toss together over a high heat until the butter melts. Serve at once.

Brussels Sprouts with Chestnuts and Shallots

Preparation Time
15 minutes
Cooking Time
12 minutes

- 900g (2lb) small Brussels sprouts, trimmed
- 1 tbsp olive oil
- 8 shallots, finely chopped
- 200g pack peeled cooked chestnuts
- 15g (½oz) butter
- a pinch of freshly grated nutmeg
- salt and ground black pepper

NUTRITIONAL INFORMATION
Per serving 140 calories,
5g fat (of which 1g saturates),
8g carbohydrate, 0.3g salt

Serves 8

Cook's Tips
If you have to store Brussels sprouts, prepare them for cooking and keep in the fridge in a polythene bag.
For convenience, blanch the Brussels sprouts ahead, then pan-fry just before serving. This helps to retain their colour and texture.

1   Add the sprouts to a large pan of lightly salted boiling water, bring back to the boil and blanch for 2 minutes. Drain the sprouts and refresh with cold water.

2   Heat the oil in a wok or sauté pan. Add the shallots and stir-fry for 5 minutes or until almost tender.

3   Add the sprouts to the pan with the chestnuts and stir-fry for about 4 minutes to heat through.

4   Add the butter and nutmeg, and season generously with salt and pepper. Serve immediately.

Quick Coronation Chicken

Preparation Time
15 minutes

- 75g (3oz) dried apricots
- 75g (3oz) sultanas
- 5 tbsp 0% fat Greek yogurt
- grated zest and juice of ½ lemon
- 1 tsp curry powder
- 4 ready-cooked chicken breasts, cut into bite-sized pieces
- 2 tbsp extra virgin olive oil
- ¾ tbsp wholegrain mustard
- 140g bag salad leaves
- salt and ground black pepper
- 1 tsp chopped fresh chives to garnish
- crusty bread to serve

NUTRITIONAL INFORMATION
Per serving 380 calories, 15g fat (of which 2g saturates), 23g carbohydrate, 0.3g salt

1 Roughly chop the apricots and put into a large bowl. Stir through the sultanas, yogurt, lemon zest, curry powder, 3 tbsp water and the cooked chicken. Check the seasoning.

2 Whisk the oil, lemon juice, mustard and some seasoning together in a small bowl. Put the salad leaves into a large serving bowl and gently toss through the dressing. Top with the chicken mixture, garnish with the chives and serve with crusty bread.

Serves 4

Super Salads

Serves 6

Goat's Cheese and Walnut Salad

Preparation Time
10 minutes

- 1 large radicchio, shredded
- 2 bunches of prepared watercress, about 125g (4oz) total weight
- 1 red onion, finely sliced
- 150g (5oz) walnut pieces
- 200g (7oz) goat's cheese, crumbled

FOR THE DRESSING
- 2 tbsp red wine vinegar
- 8 tbsp olive oil
- a large pinch of caster sugar
- salt and ground black pepper

NUTRITIONAL
INFORMATION
Per Serving 428 calories,
41g fat (of which 10g saturates),
3g carbohydrate, 0.5g salt,

1   Whisk all the ingredients for the dressing in a small bowl and put to one side.

2   Put the radicchio, watercress and onion into a large bowl. Pour the dressing over the salad and toss well.

3   To serve, divide the salad among six plates and sprinkle the walnuts and goat's cheese on top.

Grated Beetroot Salad

Preparation Time
15 minutes

- 3 large carrots
- 500g (1lb 2oz) raw beetroot
- finely grated zest and juice of 1 large orange
- 1½ tbsp runny honey
- 1 eating apple
- 50g (2oz) walnuts, roughly chopped
- a few caperberries
- a small handful of fresh flat-leafed parsley, roughly chopped
- salt and ground black pepper

NUTRITIONAL
INFORMATION
Per serving 137 calories,
6g fat (of which 1g saturates),
19g carbohydrate, 0.1g salt

1 Peel and coarsely grate the carrots and put into one half of a serving bowl. Wearing kitchen gloves to stop your hands getting stained, peel and coarsely grate the beetroot, then put into the other half of the bowl.

2 Mix the orange zest and juice, honey and some seasoning together in a small bowl.

3 Finely dice the apple (keeping skin on) and scatter over the grated vegetables, together with the chopped walnuts, caperberries and roughly chopped parsley. Drizzle over the dressing and serve.

Get Ahead
Prepare the salad to the end of step 1 up to 1 hour in advance. Cover and chill the vegetables. Cover the dressing and keep at room temperature, then complete the recipe to serve.

Serves 6

Eggs Florentine Salad

Preparation Time
15 minutes
Cooking Time
15 minutes

- 5 medium whole eggs, plus
  2 medium egg yolks
- 75g (3oz) unsalted butter
- 90g pack sliced Parma ham
- 2 English muffins, cut into
  1cm (½in) cubes
- ½ tsp English mustard
- ½ tbsp white wine vinegar
- 2 tbsp freshly chopped
  tarragon
- 225g (8oz) mix of baby
  spinach and rocket
- salt and ground black pepper

**NUTRITIONAL
INFORMATION**
Per serving 431 calories,
31g fat (of which 14g saturates),
17g carbohydrate, 1.7g salt

Serves 4

1 Bring a small pan of water to the boil. Add the whole eggs and simmer for 5 minutes. Drain, then run the eggs under cold water for 1 minute. Peel and put to one side.

2 Heat 1 tbsp of the butter in a large frying pan. Add the Parma ham and fry for 2 minutes, turning once, until golden and crisp. Drain on kitchen paper.

3 In the same pan, fry the muffin cubes until golden and crisp. Leave to drain on kitchen paper. Thickly slice the Parma ham and cut the eggs into quarters.

4 Put the raw egg yolks into a blender with the mustard and vinegar. Season well with salt and pepper. Melt the remaining butter in a small pan. With the motor of the blender running, gradually pour in the melted butter (the mixture will thicken). Empty into a bowl and stir in the tarragon.

5 Divide the spinach and rocket, the eggs, Parma ham and muffin croûtons among four plates, then spoon over the dressing. Serve immediately.

Mediterranean Salad

Preparation Time
15 minutes

- 2 × 410g cans chickpeas, drained and rinsed
- 4 tomatoes, roughly chopped
- 1 red onion, thinly sliced
- 2 small courgettes, cut into ribbons with a peeler
- 160g pack hot smoked salmon, skinned and flaked
- 50g (2oz) raisins
- 1 tbsp wholegrain mustard
- 1 tsp runny honey
- 1 tsp white wine vinegar
- 2 tbsp extra virgin olive oil
- a large handful of fresh basil
- 2 tbsp pumpkin seeds
- salt and ground black pepper

NUTRITIONAL
INFORMATION
Per serving 470 calories, 20g fat
(of which 2.5g saturates),
49g carbohydrate, 2.5g salt

Serves 4

1 Combine the chickpeas, tomatoes, onion, courgettes, salmon and raisins in a large bowl.

2 Whisk together the mustard, honey, vinegar, oil and some seasoning in a small jug. Pour the dressing over the salad and toss to coat. Sprinkle with the basil and pumpkin seeds and serve immediately.

Serves 2

Broad Bean and Feta Salad

Preparation Time
10 minutes
Cooking Time
5 minutes

- 225g (8oz) podded broad beans (see Cook's Tips)
- 100g (3½oz) feta cheese, chopped
- 2 tbsp freshly chopped mint
- 2 tbsp extra virgin olive oil
- a squeeze of lemon juice
- lemon wedges to serve (optional)
- salt and ground black pepper

NUTRITIONAL INFORMATION
Per Serving 197 calories, 16g fat (of which 4g saturates), 5g carbohydrate, 1.3g salt

1 Cook the beans in salted boiling water for 3–5 minutes until tender. Drain, then plunge into cold water and drain again. Remove their skins if you like (see Cook's Tips).

2 Tip the beans into a bowl, add the feta, mint, oil and a squeeze of lemon juice. Season well with salt and pepper and toss together. Serve with lemon wedges, if you like.

Cook's Tips
For this quantity of broad beans, you will need to buy about 750g (1½lb) beans in pods. Choose small pods, as the beans will be young and will have a better flavour than bigger, older beans.
Very young broad beans, less than 7.5cm (3in) long, can be cooked in their pods and eaten whole. Pod older beans and skin them to remove the outer coat, which toughens with age. To do this, slip the beans out of their skins after blanching. Allow about 250g (9oz) weight of whole beans in pods per person. Unless tiny, remove the beans from their pods. Cook in boiling salted water for 8–10 minutes until tender. Skin if necessary. Serve with melted butter and herbs. Older beans can be made into soup or puréed.

White Bean Salad

Preparation Time
15 minutes

- ½ tbsp red wine vinegar
- 2 tbsp extra virgin olive oil
- ½ red cabbage
- 2 courgettes
- 410g can cannellini beans, drained and rinsed
- 410g can butter beans, drained and rinsed
- ½ red onion, finely chopped
- 100g (3½oz) stale unsliced bread, torn into small chunks
- 125g ball low-fat mozzarella, torn into small pieces
- a handful of fresh basil leaves, chopped
- salt and ground black pepper

NUTRITIONAL INFORMATION
Per serving 346 calories,
13g fat (of which 5g saturates),
40g carbohydrate, 2.2g salt

1 Whisk together the vinegar, oil, plenty of seasoning and a splash of water in a small bowl to make a dressing.

2 Cut out and discard the tough core from the cabbage, then finely shred the leaves and put into a large serving bowl. Peel the courgettes into ribbons, using a y-shaped peeler, and add to the cabbage bowl. Add the remaining ingredients and dressing, and toss well to combine. Serve.

Serves 4

Serves 6

Mozzarella and Peach Salad

Preparation Time
15 minutes

- 3 ripe peaches or nectarines
- 2 × 125g (4oz) balls mozzarella, torn into bite-sized pieces
- 90g pack Parma ham slices
- 2 tbsp good-quality balsamic vinegar or balsamic glaze
- 2 tbsp clear honey
- 1 tbsp freshly choppd chives
- 40g (1½oz) skin-on almonds, roughly chopped
- rock salt and ground black pepper

NUTRITIONAL INFORMATION
Per serving 219 calories, 14g fat (of which 7g saturates), 10g carbohydrate, 2.5g salt

1 Halve the peaches or nectarines (if you're using peaches, you may want to peel them first)and remove and discard the stones. Cut each half into three wedges.

2 Divide the fruit wedges, mozzarella and the Parma ham slices among six plates.

3 Drizzle over the vinegar or balsamic glaze and honey then season with rock salt and pepper. Scatter the chives and almonds over the top and serve immediately.

Simple Winter Salad

Preparation Time
15 minutes
Cooking Time
about 10 minutes

- 110g bag salad leaves
- 1 medium pear
- 4 medium figs
- 50g (2oz) roasted hazelnuts
- 2 tbsp olive oil
- 200g (7oz) bacon lardons
- ½ tbsp wholegrain mustard
- ½ tbsp red wine vinegar
- salt and ground black pepper

NUTRITIONAL
INFORMATION
Per serving **210 calories,**
17g fat (of which **4g saturates),**
7g carbohydrate, 1.0g salt

1   Start by dividing the leaves among six plates. Next, halve, core and thinly slice the pear (leaving the skin on). Trim the figs and cut into wedges, then divide the fruit and the hazelnuts among the plates.

2   Heat 1 tbsp of the oil in a small frying pan and fry the lardons for 8 minutes until crisp and golden. Use a slotted spoon to lift them out of the pan and leave to drain on kitchen paper. Quickly make the dressing by adding the remaining oil to the pan together with the mustard, vinegar, some seasoning and a splash of water. Whisk together over a gentle heat until warmed through.

3   Divide the lardons among the plates, then drizzle over the warm dressing. Serve immediately.

Get Ahead
Fry the lardons and prepare the figs up to 1 hour in advance. Slice the pears up to 30 minutes in advance, then put in a bowl and cover. To serve, reheat the lardons and complete the recipe.

Serves 4

Provençale Tuna and Pepper Salad

Preparation Time
15 minutes
Cooking Time
about 10 minutes

- 400g (14oz) new potatoes,
  halved if large
- 200g (7oz) green beans
- 4 medium eggs
- 1 tbsp extra virgin olive oil
- grated zest and juice of
  1 lemon
- 50g (2oz) black olives, pitted
- 300g (11oz) ready-roasted red
  peppers, cut into thick strips
- 185g can tuna chunks,
  drained
- 25g pack fresh basil leaves,
  torn
- salt and ground black pepper

**NUTRITIONAL
INFORMATION**
Per serving 296 calories,
14 fat (of which 3g saturates),
23g carbohydrate, 2.3g salt

1   Bring a medium pan of water to the boil. Add the potatoes, reduce the heat and simmer for 10 minutes until tender, adding the beans for the final 4 minutes of cooking. Drain and leave to steam-dry until needed.

2   Meanwhile, bring a small pan of water to the boil, add the eggs and simmer for 8 minutes. Drain and run under cold water. Peel and quarter the eggs, then put them to one side. In a small bowl, mix together the oil, lemon zest and juice with some seasoning.

3   Put the potatoes, green beans, pitted olives, roasted pepper strips, tuna chunks and basil leaves into a large serving dish. Gently toss through the dressing (using your hands is best). Garnish with the egg quarters and serve immediately.

Warm Smoked Salmon and Cucumber Salad

Preparation Time
10 minutes
Cooking Time
about 5 minutes

- ½ tbsp vegetable oil
- 2.5cm (1in) piece fresh root ginger, peeled and finely chopped
- 1 green chilli, seeded and finely chopped (see Cook's Tips, page 46)
- 1 tbsp sesame seeds
- 6 baby sweetcorn, finely sliced
- 300g (11oz) straight-to-wok rice noodles
- 1 cucumber, peeled into ribbons
- 1 tbsp each toasted sesame oil and soy sauce
- 120g pack smoked salmon trimmings
- salt and ground black pepper
- a large handful of fresh coriander, finely chopped, to garnish
- lime wedges to serve

NUTRITIONAL
INFORMATION
Per serving 223 calories,
10g fat (of which 2g saturates),
22g carbohydrate, 1.4g salt

Serves 4

1   Heat the oil in a large frying pan or wok. Add the ginger, chilli and sesame seeds and cook for 1 minute. Stir in the baby sweetcorn and noodles and cook, stirring frequently, for 3 minutes or until noodles are tender.

2   Add the cucumber, toasted sesame oil, soy sauce and smoked salmon trimmings and heat through. Check the seasoning. Garnish with coriander and serve immediately with lime wedges to squeeze over.

King Prawn Thai-style Salad

Preparation Time
10 minutes
Cooking Time
5 minutes

- 2–3 tbsp green curry paste
- 200g (7oz) raw king prawns, peeled (see Cook's Tip, page 55)
- juice of ½ lime
- 2 large carrots and 1 cucumber, peeled into ribbons
- 100g (3½oz) fresh coconut, cubed (see Cook's Tip)
- a small handful of fresh mint, chopped
- salt and ground black pepper
- lime wedges to serve

NUTRITIONAL
INFORMATION
Per serving 308 calories,
19g fat (of which 16g saturates),
14g carbohydrate, 1.0g salt

Serves 2

Cook's Tip
Many supermarkets sell packs of fresh coconut in the chilled fruit section.

1　Heat a large frying pan, then stir in the curry paste and 1–2 tbsp hot water to loosen the paste. Cook for 30 seconds. Add the prawns and cook for 2–3 minutes until pink and cooked through.

2　Toss through the lime juice, carrots, cucumber, coconut and mint. Check the seasoning and serve with lime wedges to squeeze over.

Simple Crab Salad

Preparation Time
15 minutes
Cooking Time
about 10 minutes

- 1½ red chillies, halved, seeded and finely chopped (see Cook's Tips, page 46)
- pared zest and juice of 2 limes
- 1 tbsp wholegrain mustard
- 1 tbsp white wine vinegar
- 1 tbsp runny honey
- 100ml (3½fl oz) extra virgin olive oil
- 400g (14oz) white crabmeat
- 5 slices sourdough bread
- 2–3 tbsp olive oil
- 2 × 145g bags watercress, rocket and spinach salad
- 4 ripe avocados, stoned and thinly sliced
- 6 spring onions, finely sliced
- a small handful of fresh mint
- salt and ground black pepper

NUTRITIONAL INFORMATION
Per serving **352 calories**, **27g fat** (of which 5g saturates), **15g carbohydrate**, **0.7g salt**

GET AHEAD
Make the dressing and add the crab up to one day in advance. Cover and chill. Allow to come to room temperature, then complete the recipe to serve.

Serves 10

1 First make the dressing: mix the chillies, lime zest and juice, mustard, vinegar and honey together in a bowl. Gradually mix in the extra virgin olive oil, then stir in the crabmeat. Season to taste, then cover and chill in the fridge until needed.

2 Cut the bread into 1cm (½in) cubes. Heat 2–3 tbsp olive oil in a large frying pan, add the bread cubes and fry for 6–8 minutes until crisp. Don't overcrowd the pan or the croûtons won't crisp up (fry in batches if necessary). Season with salt and leave to cool on kitchen paper.

3 Empty the salad into a bowl, then add the sliced avocados and spring onions. Using your hands, gently toss through the crab mix.

4 Season to taste and garnish the salad with the croûtons and mint leaves before serving.

Sprouted Bean and Mango Salad

Preparation Time
15 minutes

- 3 tbsp mango chutney
- grated zest and juice of 1 lime
- 2 tbsp olive oil
- 4 plum tomatoes
- 1 small red onion, chopped
- 1 red pepper, seeded and finely diced
- 1 yellow pepper, seeded and finely diced
- 1 mango, finely diced
- 4 tbsp freshly chopped coriander
- 150g (5oz) sprouted beans (see Cook's Tip)
- salt and ground black pepper

NUTRITIONAL INFORMATION
Per Serving **103 calories,
4g fat (of which 1g saturates),
15g carbohydrate, 0.1g salt**

Cook's Tip
Many beans and seeds can be sprouted at home, but buy ones which are specifically produced for sprouting. Mung beans take five to six days to sprout. Allow 125g (4oz) bean sprouts per person. Rinse and drain. Boil or steam for 30 seconds, or stir-fry for 1–2 minutes.

Serves 6

Try Something Different
Use papaya instead of mango.
Ginger and chilli dressing Mix together 2 tsp grated fresh root ginger, 1 tbsp sweet chilli sauce, 2 tsp white wine vinegar and 2 tbsp walnut oil. Season with salt.
Peanut dressing Mix together 1 tbsp peanut butter, ¼ crushed dried chilli, 4 tsp white wine vinegar, 3 tbsp walnut oil, 1 tsp sesame oil and a dash of soy sauce.

1 To make the dressing, place the mango chutney in a small bowl and add the lime zest and juice. Whisk in the oil and season.

2 Quarter the tomatoes, discard the seeds and then dice. Put into a large bowl with the onion, peppers, mango, coriander and sprouted beans. Pour the dressing over and mix well. Serve the salad immediately.

Hot-smoked Salmon Salad

Preparation Time
15 minutes
Cooking Time
8 minutes

- 4 medium eggs
- 300g (11oz) small new potatoes, quartered
- 200g (7oz) fine green beans, trimmed and halved
- 100g (3½oz) radishes, thinly sliced
- 80g bag salad leaves
- 50g (2oz) ready-made croûtons
- 250g (9oz) hot-smoked salmon, skinned and flaked
- lemon wedges to serve

FOR THE DRESSING
- 3 tbsp sweet chilli sauce
- 1 tbsp freshly chopped chives
- 2 tbsp extra virgin olive oil
- salt and ground black pepper

NUTRITIONAL
INFORMATION
Per serving 282 calories,
11g fat (of which 2g saturates),
27g carbohydrate, 3.3g salt

1 Bring two small pans of water to the boil. To one, add the eggs and simmer for 7 minutes. To the other, add the potatoes and beans and cook for 6 minutes until just tender.

2 Meanwhile, put the radishes into a large bowl with the salad leaves, croûtons and salmon flakes. In a small bowl, mix together the dressing ingredients with some seasoning.

3 Drain the potatoes and beans and leave to steam-dry in a colander. Lift out the eggs and run under cold water then peel and quarter. Add the potatoes and beans to the salad bowl and toss gently. Divide the salad mixture among four plates and top each with a quartered egg. Drizzle over the dressing and serve with lemon wedges.

Serves 4

Chicken Caesar Salad

Preparation Time
15–20 minutes
Cooking Time
12 minutes

- 2 tbsp olive oil
- 1 garlic clove, crushed
- 2 thick slices of country-style bread, cubed
- 6 tbsp freshly grated Parmesan
- 1 cos lettuce, washed, chilled and cut into bite-size pieces
- 700g (1½lb) cooked chicken breast, sliced

FOR THE DRESSING
- 4 tbsp mayonnaise
- 2 tbsp lemon juice
- 1 tsp Dijon mustard
- 2 anchovy fillets, very finely chopped
- salt and ground black pepper

NUTRITIONAL
INFORMATION
Per serving 482 calories,
27g fat (of which 8g saturates),
8g carbohydrate, 1.4g salt

Serves 4

1 Preheat the oven to 180°C (160°C fan oven) mark 4. Put the olive oil, garlic and bread cubes in a bowl and toss well. Tip on to a baking sheet and bake in the oven for 10 minutes, turning halfway through.

2 Sprinkle the Parmesan over the croûtons and bake for 2 minutes or until the cheese has melted and the bread is golden.

3 Put all the ingredients for the dressing in a bowl, season with salt and pepper and mix.

4 Put the lettuce and sliced chicken in a bowl, pour the dressing over and toss. Top with the cheese croûtons.

Couscous and Smoked Fish Salad

Preparation Time
15 minutes
Cooking Time
about 10 minutes

- 175g (6oz) couscous
- 125g (4oz) cooked smoked fish, such as haddock, flaked
- 50g (2oz) peas, cooked
- a pinch of curry powder
- 2 spring onions, finely sliced
- 1 tbsp freshly chopped flat-leafed parsley
- 1 hard-boiled egg, chopped
- 2 tbsp olive oil
- 2 tsp lemon juice
- salt and ground black pepper

NUTRITIONAL
INFORMATION
Per serving 219 calories,
9g fat (of which 2g saturates),
24g carbohydrate, 0.5g salt

Serves 4

1   Cook the couscous according to the pack instructions.

2   Put the cooked couscous into a large serving bowl, then use a fork to break it up and separate the grains.

3   Add the smoked fish, cooked peas, curry powder, spring onions, parsley, egg, olive oil and lemon juice, stirring gently to combine. Check the seasoning and serve.

Serves 6

Stilton and Fig Salad

Preparation Time
15 minutes

- 12 figs, woody stalks trimmed
- 6 slices Parma ham, halved lengthways
- 1 punnet of cress
- 100g (3½oz) radishes
- 40g (1½oz) Stilton, roughly crumbled
- 3 tbsp balsamic glaze
- 3 tbsp runny honey
- 3 tbsp extra virgin olive oil
- ground black pepper
- crusty bread to serve

NUTRITIONAL INFORMATION
Per serving: 206 calories,
12g fat (of which 4g saturates),
17g carbohydrate, 1.0g salt

1 Put a fig base down on a board and cut vertically into quarters, leaving them attached at the base. Use your fingers to press the base of the fig to open up the quarters. Repeat with the rremaining figs.

2 Wrap a Parma ham strip around the base of each fig and put to one side. Trim the cress from the soil and discard the soil, then thinly slice the radishes.

3 Place two figs on each of the six plates. Divide the radishes, cress and Stilton equally among the plates. Drizzle ½ tbsp each of the balsamic glaze, honey and oil over each plate, season with pepper and serve with crusty bread.

Get Ahead
Complete the recipe to the end of step 2 up to 3 hours in advance. Cover and chill the figs. Put the cress and radishes into separate bowls, cover with damp kitchen paper, then cover and chill. Bring to room temperature and complete the recipe to serve.

Orange and Smoked Mackerel Salad

Preparation Time
15 minutes

FOR THE SALAD
- 300g (11oz) smoked mackerel
- 2 oranges
- 1 large courgette, cut into ribbons with a peeler
- 100g bag watercress
- 40g (1½oz) flaked almonds
- crusty bread to serve (optional)

FOR THE DRESSING
- 1 tsp wholegrain mustard
- 1 tsp honey or sugar
- 2 tbsp white wine vinegar
- 4 tbsp extra virgin olive oil
- salt and ground black pepper

NUTRITIONAL
INFORMATION
Per serving 475 calories,
40g fat (of which 7g saturates),
10g carbohydrate, 1.5g salt

Serves 4

Cook's Tip
Make a large batch of the dressing and keep in a sealed jar in the fridge for up to a month, ready to pour over salads whenever you like.

1   Peel the skin off the mackerel and discard. Flake the mackerel into a large serving bowl. Slice the peel and pith off the oranges and cut horizontally (across segments) into slices, then cut each slice in half to make two semi-circles. Discard the pips. Add to the mackerel, together with the courgette ribbons, watercress and most of the almonds.

2   Mix the dressing ingredients together in a small bowl with some seasoning. Drizzle over the salad and toss together lightly. Sprinkle over the remaining almonds and serve with some crusty bread, if you like.

Melon and Chorizo Salad

Preparation Time
10 minutes
Cooking Time
about 8 minutes

- 1 cantaloupe melon
- 75ml (3fl oz) balsamic vinegar
- 1 tbsp runny honey
- 75g (3oz) chorizo, in one piece, skinned
- 1 tbsp oil
- 1 punnet of cress, trimmed
- crusty bread to serve (optional)

NUTRITIONAL INFORMATION
Per serving 98 calories,
5g fat (of which 2g saturates),
11g carbohydrate, 0.2g salt

Serves 6

Get Ahead
Prepare the recipe to the end of step 3 up to 2 hours in advance. Cover the balsamic glaze and chorizo oil and keep at room temperature. Cover the melon and chorizo and chill. Allow the chorizo to come up to room temperature before completing recipe to serve.

1 Halve the melon, then spoon out and discard the seeds. Cut each half into three wedges, then cut the skin off each wedge and chill until needed.

2 Put the balsamic vinegar and honey into a small pan and simmer gently for 5 minutes until syrupy. Leave to cool.

3 Cut the chorizo into small cubes. Heat the oil in a small frying pan and add the sausage cubes. Fry for 3 minutes until the chorizo is golden. Strain into a small bowl and put the oil and chorizo to one side.

4 Put a melon wedge on each of six small plates, then sprinkle over some of the fried chorizo and cress. Finally, drizzle the chorizo oil and balsamic glaze over each plate. Serve immediately with crusty bread, if you like.

Italian-style Steak Salad

Preparation Time
10 minutes
Cooking Time
10 minutes, plus resting

- 2 × 250g (9oz) rump steaks, fat trimmed
- 1 tbsp extra virgin olive oil, plus extra to drizzle (optional)
- 2–3 tbsp fresh pesto, to taste
- 110g bag salad leaves
- 250g (9oz) cherry tomatoes
- 100g (3½oz) marinated artichoke pieces from a jar, drained
- 50g (2oz) toasted pinenuts
- 25g (1oz) Parmesan cheese shavings
- salt and ground black pepper
- crusty bread to serve

NUTRITIONAL
INFORMATION
Per Serving 378 calories,
25g fat (of which 6g saturates),
3g carbohydrate, 1.1g salt

1 Pat the steaks dry with kitchen paper, then season well on both sides. Heat the oil in a large frying pan over a high heat and fry the steaks for 5 minutes, turning once, for medium rare (cook for longer or shorter depending on your preference).

2 Meanwhile, in a small bowl, stir together the pesto, some black pepper and enough water to make a loose dressing. Put the salad leaves, tomatoes and artichoke pieces into a large serving bowl, then pour over most of the pesto dressing and toss to combine.

3 When the steaks are cooked, transfer to a board and leave to rest for 5 minutes before slicing into strips. Add the steak strips to the salad, then drizzle over the remaining pesto dressing and some extra oil, if you like. Sprinkle the pinenuts and Parmesan shavings over the top and serve immediately with crusty bread.

Serves 4

Serves 4

Spring Lamb and Flageolet Bean Salad

Preparation Time
5 minutes
Cooking Time
10–20 minutes, plus resting

- 2–3 lamb fillets, about 700g (1½lb) in total
- 1 tbsp Dijon mustard
- 5 tbsp olive oil
- 1 tsp freshly chopped parsley
- 2 garlic cloves
- juice of 1 lemon
- 400g can flageolet or cannellini beans, drained and rinsed
- 125g (4oz) frisée lettuce or curly endive
- 250g (9oz) baby plum or cherry tomatoes, halved
- salt and ground black pepper

NUTRITIONAL INFORMATION
Per Serving 535 calories, 35g fat (of which 11g saturates), 17g carbohydrate, 1.4g salt

1 Rub the lamb fillets with the mustard and season with pepper. Put 1 tbsp oil in a non-stick frying pan and fry the lamb over a medium heat for 5–7 minutes on each side for medium-rare, 8–10 minutes for well done. Remove the lamb, cover and put to one side for 5 minutes. This allows the meat to relax, which makes slicing easier.

2 To make the dressing, put the parsley, garlic, lemon juice and remaining oil into a food processor and whiz for 10 seconds. Alternatively, put the ingredients into a screw-topped jar, screw on the lid and shake to combine.

3 Put the beans, frisée or curly endive and the tomatoes into a bowl, combine with the dressing and season to taste with salt and pepper.

4 Slice the lamb into 1cm (½in) pieces and place on top of the flageolet salad. Serve immediately.

Try Something Different
For a vegetarian alternative, skewer the whole tomatoes on soaked wooden kebab sticks, alternating with small balls of mozzarella cheese. Grill the kebabs and drizzle with 2 tbsp pesto sauce thinned with a little olive oil.

Pasta Dishes

Serves 4

Spaghetti alla Carbonara

Preparation Time
10 minutes
Cooking Time
10 minutes

- 2 tbsp olive oil
- 25g (1oz) butter
- 125–150g (4–5oz) smoked pancetta (see Cook's Tips), rind removed, cut into strips
- 1 garlic clove, halved
- 3 medium eggs
- 2 tbsp dry white wine
- 40g (1½oz) freshly grated Parmesan
- 40g (1½oz) freshly grated Pecorino cheese
- 400g (14oz) dried spaghetti
- salt and ground black pepper
- 2 tbsp freshly chopped parsley to garnish

NUTRITIONAL INFORMATION
Per Serving 750 calories, 38g fat (of which 12g saturates), 74g carbohydrate, 2.2g salt

1 Heat the oil and butter in a heavy-based pan. Add the pancetta and garlic, and cook over a medium heat for 3–4 minutes until the pancetta begins to crisp. Turn off the heat; discard the garlic.

2 Meanwhile, in a bowl, beat the eggs with the white wine and half each of the cheeses. Season with salt and pepper.

3 Cook the spaghetti in a large pan of boiling salted water according to the pack instructions until it is al dente.

4 When the spaghetti is almost cooked, gently reheat the pancetta in the pan.

5 Drain the spaghetti thoroughly, then return to the pan. Immediately add the egg mixture together with the pancetta. Take the pan off the heat and toss well; the eggs will cook in the residual heat to form a light creamy sauce. Add the remaining cheeses, toss lightly and serve immediately garnished with parsley.

Cook's Tips
If smoked pancetta is unobtainable, use smoked bacon instead, increasing the quantity to 175–225g (6–8oz).
If Pecorino is unobtainable, just double the quantity of the Parmesan.

Ribbon Pasta with Courgettes

Preparation Time
about 5 minutes
Cooking Time
8–10 minutes

- 450g (1lb) pappardelle pasta
- 2 large courgettes, coarsely grated
- 1 red chilli, seeded and finely chopped (see Cook's Tips, page 46)
- 2 tbsp salted capers, rinsed
- 1 garlic clove, crushed
- 4 tbsp pitted black Kalamata olives, roughly chopped
- 4 tbsp extra virgin olive oil
- 2 tbsp freshly chopped flat-leafed parsley
- salt and ground black pepper
- freshly grated Parmesan to serve (see Cook's Tip)

NUTRITIONAL
INFORMATION
Per Serving 518 calories,
15g fat (of which 2g saturates),
86g carbohydrate, 1.7g salt

1 Cook the pappardelle in a large pan of boiling water until al dente. About 1 minute before the end of the cooking time, add the courgettes, then simmer until the pasta is just cooked.

2 Meanwhile, put the chilli, capers, garlic, olives and oil in a small pan. Stir over a low heat for 2–3 minutes.

3 Drain the pasta and put back in the pan. Pour the hot caper mixture on top, mix well and toss with the parsley. Season with salt and pepper and serve immediately with the Parmesan.

Try Something Different
If cooking for non-vegetarians, try this variation. Omit the Parmesan cheese and in step 2, add a 50g can of anchovies, drained and roughly chopped.

Cook's Tip
Traditional Parmesan cheese contains animal rennet, but you can now buy vegetarian-style Parmesan cheese in most major supermarkets.

Serves 4

Serves 4

Chilli Squid Linguine

Preparation Time
15 minutes
Cooking Time
about 15 minutes

- 350g (12oz) dried linguine pasta
- 1 tbsp extra virgin olive oil, plus extra to drizzle
- 1 garlic clove, finely chopped
- ½–1 red chilli, to taste, seeded and finely chopped (see Cook's Tips, page 46)
- 400g (14oz) baby squid, cleaned and sliced into rings
- 1 tbsp capers, rinsed
- finely grated zest and juice of 1 lemon
- a small handful of fresh mint, chopped
- a large handful of rocket
- salt and ground black pepper

NUTRITIONAL INFORMATION

Per serving 412 calories, 6g fat (of which 1g saturates), 68g carbohydrate, 0.6g salt

1 Bring a large pan of salted water to the boil and cook the pasta according to the pack instructions. Drain the cooked pasta, reserving a cupful of the cooking water.

2 Heat the oil in a large frying pan over a high heat and fry the garlic and chilli for 10 seconds before adding the squid and capers. Fry for 1 minute to colour and cook the squid, then add the cooked pasta, lemon zest and juice, the chopped mint and rocket, and toss to combine. Add a little of the reserved pasta water if the mixture is too dry. Season well with salt and pepper and serve drizzled with a little extra olive oil, if you like.

Broccoli and Courgette Shells

Preparation Time
15 minutes
Cooking Time
about 10 minutes

◆ 400g (14oz) dried conchiglie
◆ 250g (9oz) broccoli florets
◆ 25g (1oz) butter
◆ 1 garlic clove, finely chopped
◆ 2 courgettes, grated
◆ grated zest and juice of
  ½ lemon
◆ 3 tbsp red pesto
◆ a large handful of fresh
  parsley, roughly chopped
◆ salt and ground black pepper
◆ 15g (½oz) flaked almonds,
  toasted, to garnish

**NUTRITIONAL
INFORMATION**
Per serving 439 calories,
13g fat (of which 4g saturates),
68g carbohydrate, 0.3g salt

1 Bring a large pan of salted water to the boil and cook the pasta according to the pack instructions. Drain.

2 Meanwhile, cook the broccoli in a pan of boiling water for 3 minutes, then drain and put to one side.

3 Heat the butter in a non-stick frying pan and fry the garlic for 1 minute. Stir in the grated courgettes and fry for a further 3 minutes, stirring frequently. Add the lemon zest and juice, the pesto, parsley and some seasoning, then mix in the broccoli and hot cooked pasta. Garnish with the toasted almonds.

Serves 4

Thai Green Prawn Curry Pasta

Preparation Time
10 minutes
Cooking Time
18 minutes

- 400g (14oz) dried farfalle
- 1 tbsp sunflower oil
- 1 leek, trimmed and thinly sliced
- 1 tsp Thai green curry paste
- 1½ × 400ml cans coconut milk
- ½ tbsp fish sauce
- 300g (11oz) raw king prawns, peeled (see Cook's Tip, page 55)
- 125g (4oz) frozen peas
- freshly chopped coriander to garnish

NUTRITIONAL
INFORMATION
Per serving 713 calories,
32g fat (of which 1g saturates),
81g carbohydrate, 0.6g salt

Serves 4

1 Bring a large pan of salted water to the boil and cook the pasta according to the pack instructions. Drain.

2 Meanwhile, heat the oil in a large pan and gently fry the leek for 10 minutes until softened. Stir in the curry paste and cook for 1 minute. Add the coconut milk and fish sauce and simmer for 5 minutes. Stir in the prawns and peas and cook until the prawns turn bright pink.

3 Divide the hot cooked pasta among four warmed bowls and top with the sauce. Garnish with chopped coriander and serve.

Bacon, Chilli and Sage Pasta

Preparation Time
10 minutes
Cooking Time
about 5 minutes

- 400g (14oz) dried fusilli
- 150g (5oz) smoked streaky bacon, chopped
- 50g (2oz) butter
- 1 tbsp finely chopped sage
- ½ red chilli, seeded and finely chopped (see Cook's Tips, page 46)
- ground black pepper

NUTRITIONAL INFORMATION
Per serving 576 calories,
25g fat (of which 10g saturates),
75g carbohydrate, 1.4g salt

Serves 4

1 Bring a large pan of salted water to the boil and cook the pasta according to the pack instructions. Drain.

2 Meanwhile, heat a large pan and fry the bacon for 3 minutes. Add the butter, chopped sage and chilli and cook for a further 30 seconds.

3 Season with pepper, then stir into the hot cooked pasta and serve.

Serves 4

Lentil and Bacon Pasta

Preparation Time
10 minutes
Cooking Time
about 10 minutes

- 400g (14oz) dried rigatoni
- 1 tbsp olive oil
- 2 shallots, sliced
- 125g (4oz) smoked streaky bacon, sliced
- 1 garlic clove, crushed
- 1 tbsp fresh oregano leaves
- 1½ × 250g packs ready-to-eat Puy lentils
- 300ml (½ pint) hot chicken stock
- freshly chopped curly parsley and basil to garnish
- salt and ground black pepper

NUTRITIONAL INFORMATION
Per serving **562 calories,**
13g fat (of which 3g saturates),
91g carbohydrate, 2.2g salt

1 Bring a large pan of salted water to the boil and cook the pasta according to the pack instructions. Drain.

2 Meanwhile, heat the oil in a pan add the shallots and bacon and fry for 3 minutes. Stir in the garlic and oregano and cook for a further 1 minute. Add the Puy lentils then pour in the hot stock and simmer for 5-7 minutes. Season with salt and pepper.

3 Stir through the hot cooked pasta, garnish with chopped parsley and basil and serve immediately.

Courgette and Fennel Pasta

Preparation Time
10 minutes
Cooking Time
about 10 minutes

◆ 400g (14oz) fusilli pasta
◆ 25g (1oz) butter
◆ 50g (2oz) pinenuts
◆ 1 large fennel, thinly sliced
◆ 2 large courgettes, grated
◆ finely grated zest and juice
  of 1 lemon
◆ 150ml (5fl oz) double cream
◆ 3 tbsp finely chopped dill
◆ salt and ground black pepper
◆ Parmesan shavings to serve

**NUTRITIONAL
INFORMATION**
Per serving **688 calories,
37g fat (of which 17g saturates),
77g carbohydrate, 0.2g salt**

1 Bring a large pan of salted water to the boil and cook the pasta according to the pack instructions. Drain.

2 Meanwhile, melt the butter in a large frying pan and toast the pinenuts for 2 minutes until golden. Add the fennel and cook for 5 minutes until starting to soften. Stir in the courgettes and cook for 3–5 minutes until the vegetables are tender.

3 Add the lemon zest and juice, cream, dill and drained pasta to the pan and stir to combine. Check the seasoning and serve immediately topped with Parmesan shavings.

Serves 4

Balsamic Chicken Pasta

Preparation Time
15 minutes
Cooking Time
about 15 minutes

- 350g (12oz) conchiglie pasta
- 200g (7oz) green beans, trimmed and cut in half
- 3 skinless chicken breasts, cut into strips
- ½ tbsp olive oil
- 1 red onion, finely chopped
- 1 garlic clove, finely chopped
- 2 tbsp good-quality balsamic vinegar
- 300g (11oz) cherry tomatoes
- 2 tbsp each roughly chopped basil and parsley
- salt and ground black pepper

NUTRITIONAL INFORMATION
Per serving 477 calories,
5g fat (of which 1g saturates),
72g carbohydrate, 0.2g salt

Serves 4

1 Bring a large pan of salted water to the boil and cook the pasta according to the pack instructions. Add the beans for last 4 minutes. Drain.

2 Meanwhile, put the chicken strips in a pan and cover with cold water. Bring to the boil, reduce the heat and simmer for 5 minutes or until cooked through. Drain.

3 Heat the oil in a large frying pan, add the onion and gently cook for 5 minutes until softened and beginning to caramelise – add a splash of water if the pan starts to dry out. Add the garlic, vinegar, cherry tomatoes and some seasoning and cook for 1 minute, then briefly whiz in a blender.

4 Drain the pasta and toss with the chicken and sauce. Stir through most of the herbs and season. Sprinkle with remaining herbs and serve immediately.

Spring Onion, Pea and Mint Penne

Preparation Time
10 minutes
Cooking Time
about 10 minutes

Serves 4

- ◆ 350g (12oz) dried penne
- ◆ 200g (7oz) frozen peas
- ◆ 1 tbsp olive oil
- ◆ 80g pack prosciutto, roughly chopped
- ◆ 6 spring onions, sliced
- ◆ 1 garlic clove, crushed
- ◆ 4 tbsp double cream
- ◆ 2 tbsp freshly chopped mint
- ◆ 25g (1oz) Parmesan, grated
- ◆ salt and ground black pepper

NUTRITIONAL INFORMATION
Per serving **519 calories**, 18g fat (of which 8g saturates), 71g carbohydrate, 0.7g salt

1 Bring a large pan of salted water to the boil and cook the pasta according to the pack instructions. Add the peas for the last 4 minutes.

2 Meanwhile, heat the oil in a large pan and gently fry the prosciutto and spring onions for 3 minutes. Add the garlic and cook for 1 minute.

3 Drain the pasta, reserving 50–75ml (2–3fl oz) of the cooking water. Add the pasta to the onion mixture with the cream, mint and enough of the reserved water to make a sauce. Toss well, then divide among four warmed bowls. Sprinkle with Parmesan and lots of pepper and serve immediately.

Pasta with Blue Cheese and Spinach

Preparation Time
about 10 minutes
Cooking Time
10 minutes

◆ 400g (14oz) rigatoni pasta
◆ 150ml (5fl oz) milk
◆ 200g (7oz) half-fat crème fraîche
◆ 75g (3oz) Gorgonzola, crumbled
◆ 75g (3oz) chopped sun-blush tomatoes
◆ 1 red chilli, seeded and chopped (see Cook's Tips, page 46)
◆ a large handful of baby leaf spinach
◆ salt and ground black pepper

NUTRITIONAL INFORMATION
Per serving 620 calories,
27g fat (of which 12g saturates),
79g carbohydrate, 0.4g salt

Serves 4

1 Bring a large pan of salted water to the boil and cook the pasta according to the pack instructions.

2 Meanwhile, put the milk into a pan and bring to a simmer. Take off the heat and whisk in the crème fraîche and half the Gorgonzola. Season to taste with lots of pepper.

3 Drain the pasta thoroughly, tip back into the pan and toss through the sun-blush tomatoes, chilli, spinach and remaining Gorgonzola. Drizzle the cheese sauce generously over the top of the pasta and serve immediately.

Very Easy Four-cheese Gnocchi

Preparation Time
3 minutes
Cooking Time
10 minutes

- ◆ 350g pack fresh gnocchi
- ◆ 300g tub fresh four-cheese sauce
- ◆ 240g pack sunblush tomatoes
- ◆ 2 tbsp freshly torn basil leaves, plus basil sprigs to garnish
- ◆ 1 tbsp freshly grated Parmesan (see Cook's Tip, page 120)
- ◆ 15g (½oz) butter, chopped
- ◆ salt and ground black pepper
- ◆ salad to serve

NUTRITIONAL INFORMATION
Per Serving 630 calories,
28g fat (of which 15g saturates),
77g carbohydrate, 5.7g salt

Serves 2

1 Cook the gnocchi in a large pan of lightly salted boiling water according to the pack instructions, or until all the gnocchi have floated to the surface. Drain well and put the gnocchi back into the pan.

2 Preheat the grill. Add the four-cheese sauce and tomatoes to the gnocchi and heat gently, stirring, for 2 minutes.

3 Season with salt and pepper, then add the basil and stir again. Spoon into individual heatproof bowls, sprinkle a little Parmesan over each one and dot with the butter.

4 Cook under the hot grill for 3–5 minutes until golden and bubbling. Garnish with basil sprigs and serve with salad.

Serves 4

Gnocchi Bake

Preparation Time
5 minutes
Cooking Time
about 10 minutes

- 750g (1lb 11oz) gnocchi
- 3 tbsp mascarpone
- 400g can cherry tomatoes
- ½ tbsp sun-dried tomato purée
- 1 spring onion, thinly sliced
- ½ garlic clove, finely chopped
- 125g ball buffalo mozzarella, torn into pieces
- a large handful of rocket
- salt and ground black pepper

NUTRITIONAL INFORMATION
Per serving 440 calories,
12g fat (of which 8g saturates),
68g carbohydrate, 2.8g salt

1 Preheat the grill to medium. Cook the gnocchi in a large pan of lightly salted water to the boil for 3–4 minutes or until they float to the surface. Drain well and tip the gnocchi into a large bowl.

2 Stir through the mascarpone, tomatoes, tomato purée, spring onion and garlic. Check the seasoning, then transfer the mixture to a 2 litre (3½ pint) ovenproof casserole dish. Dot over the mozzarella, then put under the grill for 5 minutes or until piping hot and golden. Top with rocket and serve.

Pesto Gnocchi

Preparation Time
10 minutes
Cooking Time
about 10 minutes

- 2 × 500g bags gnocchi
- 4 tbsp fresh pesto
- 400g (14oz) mascarpone
- 1 red chilli, seeded and finely chopped (see Cook's Tips, page 46), plus extra to garnish (optional)
- salt and ground black pepper
- a large handful of fresh basil, roughly chopped, to garnsih

NUTRITIONAL INFORMATION
Per serving 600 calories, 37g fat (of which 11g saturates), 57g carbohydrate, 3.0g salt

Serves 6

1 Cook the gnocchi in a large pan of lightly salted boiling water according to the pack instructions, or until all the gnocchi have floated to the surface.

2 Meanwhile, mix the pesto, mascarpone, chilli and some seasoning together in a medium bowl. Drain well and put the gnocchi back into the pan. Stir in the mascarpone mixture and check the seasoning. Garnish with extra chopped chilli, if you like, and the basil. Serve immediately.

Fennel and Sausage Gnocchi

Preparation Time
10 minutes
Cooking Time
about 20 minutes

- 1 tbsp olive oil
- 1 onion, finely chopped
- 1 fennel bulb, finely sliced
- 8 good-quality pork sausage, about 450g (1lb)
- 2 × 350g jars of pasta sauce, such as tomato and basil pasta sauce
- 2 × 500g packs gnocchi
- a large handful each of fresh basil and rocket
- salt and ground black pepper
- grated Parmesan to garnish (optional)

NUTRITIONAL INFORMATION
Per serving 498 calories,
16g fat (of which 5g saturates),
70g carbohydrate, 5.1g salt

Serves 6

1 Heat the oil in a large frying pan over a medium heat. Add the onion and fennel and fry for 6 minutes or until beginning to soften. Meanwhile, peel off and discard the sausage skins. Add the sausages to the pan (breaking up the meat with a wooden spoon) and continue cooking for about 8 minutes until golden. Pour in the pasta sauce and simmer for 3 minutes until piping hot.

2 Meanwhile, cook the gnocchi in a large pan of lightly salted boiling water according to the pack instructions or until they float to the surface. Drain well and put the gnocchi back into the pan. Pour the sausage sauce over the gnocchi and stir through most of the basil and rocket. Check the seasoning. Divide among six warmed bowls and garnish with the remaining basil and rocket and some grated Parmesan, if you like.

Japanese Pork with Vermicelli

Preparation Time
10 minutes, plus standing
Cooking Time
about 20 minutes

- ½ tbsp miso paste
- 400g (14oz) pork fillet
- ½ tbsp sunflower oil
- 1 small red chilli, seeded and finely chopped (see Cook's Tips, page 46)
- 1 tbsp each rice wine vinegar and fish sauce
- 200ml (7fl oz) hot chicken stock
- 2 heads pak choi, about 225g (8oz)
- 250g (9oz) rice noodles
- 4 spring onions, roughly sliced
- a large handful of fresh coriander, roughly chopped

NUTRITIONAL
INFORMATION
Per serving 406 calories,
9g fat (of which 3g saturates),
53g carbohydrate, 1.0g salt

1 Brush the miso over the pork. Heat the oil in a non-stick frying pan and brown the meat all over. Add the chilli and cook for a further 1 minute. Pour in the vinegar, fish sauce and hot stock, then cover and simmer for 10 minutes until cooked. Remove the pork and rest on a board, loosely covered with foil. Keep the sauce warm.

2 Meanwhile, divide the pak choi into leaves. Put the small leaves to one side and roughly shred the remainder. Put all the leaves into a bowl and cover with boiling water. Leave to soften for 10 minutes.

3 Cook the noodles for 2–3 minutes in boiling water, then strain. Divide among four bowls. Thinly slice the pork and arrange in the bowls with the drained pak choi. Ladle over the warm sauce, garnish with the spring onions and coriander and serve.

Serves 4

Serves 4

Cheat's Macaroni Cheese

Preparation Time
10 minutes
Cooking Time
about 10 minutes

- 300g (11oz) dried macaroni
- 300g pack cauliflower and broccoli florets (or ½ small head each broccoli and cauliflower), cut into smaller florets
- 300g (11oz) low-fat cream cheese
- 150g (5oz) mature Cheddar cheese, grated
- ½ tsp English mustard
- 1 tbsp freshly chopped chives, plus extra to garnish
- 25g (1oz) dried breadcrumbs
- salt and ground black pepper
- green salad to serve

NUTRITIONAL INFORMATION
Per serving 564 calories,
21g fat (of which 12g saturates),
66g carbohydrate, 1.0g salt

1 Bring a large pan of water to the boil and cook the pasta according to the pack instructions. Add the vegetables for the last 3 minutes. Drain and put back into the pan.

2 Meanwhile, put the cream cheese and most of the Cheddar into a small pan and heat gently to melt, then stir in the mustard, chives and some salt and pepper. Stir the sauce into the drained pasta pan and check the seasoning. Add a little water if you prefer a thinner sauce.

3 Preheat the grill to medium. Divide the macaroni mixture among four individual heatproof dishes, then put them on a baking sheet. Sprinkle the remaining cheese and the breadcrumbs over the dishes, then season with pepper. Grill for 5 minutes or until golden and bubbling. Garnish with chives and serve with a green salad.

Courgette and Goat's Cheese Spaghetti

Preparation Time
10 minutes
Cooking Time
about 10 minutes

- 350g (12oz) dried spaghetti
- 1 tbsp olive oil
- 1 garlic clove, finely chopped
- ½–1 red chilli, to taste, seeded and finely chopped (see Cook's Tips, page 46)
- 2 medium courgettes, coarsely grated
- finely grated zest and juice of 1 lemon
- 75g (3oz) soft, crumbly goat's cheese
- a small handful of fresh mint, finely shredded
- salt and ground black pepper

NUTRITIONAL
INFORMATION
Per serving **393 calories,**
9g fat (of which 4g saturates),
66g carbohydrate, 0.3g salt

1   Cook the spaghetti in a large pan of boiling water according to the pack instructions.

2   Meanwhile, heat the oil in a large frying pan, add the garlic and chilli and fry for 30 seconds, then add the courgette and fry for a further 1 minute. Put to one side.

3   When the pasta is cooked to your liking, reserve a cupful of the cooking water before draining. Add the drained pasta to the courgette pan together with the lemon zest and juice. Crumble in most of the goat's cheese, then toss to combine, adding some of the reserved pasta water if the mixture seems dry.

4   Check the seasoning, then divide among four bowls. Sprinkle over the mint, remaining goat's cheese and plenty of pepper. Serve immediately.

Serves 4

Serves 4

Seafood, Artichoke and Mint Pasta

Preparation Time
10 minutes
Cooking Time
about 10 minutes

- ◆ 400g (14oz) pasta tubes or twists
- ◆ 2 tbsp olive oil
- ◆ 1 small red onion, finely chopped
- ◆ 150g (5oz) marinated artichokes, roughly chopped
- ◆ 300g (11oz) seafood cocktail
- ◆ juice of ½ lemon
- ◆ 2 tbsp finely chopped mint
- ◆ salt and ground black pepper

NUTRITIONAL INFORMATION
Per serving **505 calories,**
12g fat (of which 2g saturates),
80g carbohydrate, 2.1g salt

1 Bring a large pan of salted water to the boil and cook the pasta according to the pack instructions. Drain.

2 Meanwhile, heat the oil in a pan, add the onion and fry for 10 minutes. Stir in the artichokes and seafood cocktail. Heat through, then add the lemon juice and mint. Check the seasoning, then stir into the hot cooked pasta and serve immediately.

Mushroom Linguine

Preparation Time
15 minutes
Cooking Time
about 10 minutes

- 400g (14oz) linguine
- 15g (½oz) butter
- 350g (12oz) chestnut mushrooms, sliced
- 25g (1oz) pinenuts
- 1 tbsp brandy (optional)
- 100g (3½oz) mascarpone
- 40g (1½oz) Parmesan, grated, plus extra to garnish
- finely grated zest of 1 lemon
- a large handful of baby spinach
- salt and ground black pepper

NUTRITIONAL INFORMATION
Per serving 582 calories,
23g fat (of which 12g saturates),
76g carbohydrate, 0.5g salt

Serves 4

1   Bring a large pan of salted water to the boil and cook the pasta according to the pack instructions. Drain, reserving 150ml (5fl oz) cooking water.

2   Meanwhile, heat the butter in a large frying pan over a high heat. Add the mushrooms and cook for 3–5 minutes. Add the pinenuts and cook for a further 1 minute. Stir in the brandy (if using) and bubble for 1 minute.

3   Add the mascarpone, Parmesan, cooking water and lemon zest to the pan, then stir in the spinach and linguini and heat through. Check the seasoning, garnish with extra Parmesan and serve.

Pasta with Leeks, Pancetta and Mushrooms

Preparation Time
5 minutes
Cooking Time
15–20 minutes

Serves 4

- 450g (1lb) dried conchiglie pasta
- 50g (2oz) butter
- 125g (4oz) pancetta, diced
- 2 medium leeks, thickly sliced
- 225g (8oz) chestnut mushrooms, sliced
- 1 garlic clove, crushed
- 150g pack soft cream cheese with herbs
- salt and ground black pepper
- basil leaves to garnish

NUTRITIONAL INFORMATION
Per serving 765 calories, 39g fat (of which 22g saturates), 86g carbohydrate, 1.5g salt

1 Cook the pasta according to the pack instructions until al dente.

2 Meanwhile, melt the butter in a pan and add the pancetta, leeks, mushrooms and garlic. Cook over a medium heat for 5–10 minutes until the leeks are tender. Reduce the heat, add the cream cheese and season well with salt and pepper.

3 Drain the pasta, add to the sauce and toss well. Garnish with basil and serve.

Fish Suppers

Serves 4

Special Prawn Fried Rice

Preparation Time

Cooking Time

- 2 × 250g packs of microwavable rice (see Cook's Tips)
- 1 tbsp sesame oil
- 6 tbsp nasi goreng paste (see Cook's Tips)
- 200g (7oz) green cabbage, shredded
- 250g (9oz) cooked and peeled large prawns
- 2 tbsp light soy sauce
- 1 tbsp sunflower oil
- 2 medium eggs, beaten
- 2 spring onions, thinly sliced
- 1 lime, cut into wedges, to serve

NUTRITIONAL INFORMATION
Per Serving 412 calories, 18g fat (of which 3g saturates), 46g carbohydrate, 1.9g salt

1 Cook the rice according to the pack instructions.

2 Heat the sesame oil in a wok and fry the nasi goreng paste for 1–2 minutes. Add the cabbage and stir-fry for 2–3 minutes. Add the prawns and stir briefly, then add the rice and soy sauce and cook for a further 5 minutes, stirring occasionally.

3 To make the omelette, heat the sunflower oil in a non-stick frying pan (about 25.5cm/10in in diameter) and add the eggs. Swirl around to cover the base of the pan in a thin layer and cook for 2–3 minutes until set.

4 Roll up the omelette and cut it into strips. Serve the rice scattered with the omelette and spring onions and pass round the lime wedges to squeeze over it.

Cook's Tips
If you can't find microwavable rice, use 200g (7oz) longgrain rice, cooked according to the pack instructions – but do not overcook. Rinse in cold water and drain well before you begin the recipe. Nasi goreng is a spicy Indonesian dish traditionally eaten for breakfast. Nasi goreng paste can be bought at most large supermarkets and Asian food shops.

Chilli King Prawns

Preparation Time
10 minutes, plus marinating

- 400g (14oz) cooked king prawns, thawed if frozen
- pared zest and juice of 2 limes
- ½ green chilli, seeded and finely chopped (see Cook's Tips, page 46)
- ½ tbsp poppy seeds
- ½ tbsp caster sugar
- 2 tbsp extra virgin olive oil
- 125g (4oz) cherry tomatoes, halved
- 4 spring onions, thinly sliced
- a large handful of fresh coriander, roughly chopped
- salt and ground black pepper
- lime wedges and Easy Noodles (see page 210) to serve

NUTRITIONAL INFORMATION
Per serving 106 calories,
6g fat (of which 1g saturates),
2g carbohydrate, 2.5g salt

Serves 6

1 Put the prawns, lime zest and juice, chilli, poppy seeds, sugar, oil and tomatoes into a large bowl. Season with salt and pepper, then cover and chill for up to 2 hours to let the flavours mingle.

2 Mix in the spring onions and coriander and check the seasoning. Serve with lime wedges and Easy Noodles.

Our Favourite Curry

Preparation Time

Cooking Time

- 1 tbsp vegetable oil
- 1 large onion, finely chopped
- 1 garlic clove, crushed
- 4cm (1½in) piece fresh root ginger, peeled and grated
- 1–2 green chillies, seeded and finely chopped (see Cook's Tips, page 46)
- ¼ tsp ground turmeric
- 1 tsp each ground coriander and ground cumin
- 160ml can coconut cream
- 100ml (3½fl oz) fish stock
- 500g (1lb 2oz) fresh tomatoes, roughly chopped
- 400g (14oz) raw king prawns (see Cook's Tip, page 55)
- salt and ground black pepper
- 2 tbsp freshly chopped coriander to garnish

TO SERVE
- boiled basmati rice or naan
- lime wedges
- chutney

NUTRITIONAL
INFORMATION
Per serving 330 calories,
23g fat (of which 14g saturates),
10g carbohydrate, 0.5g salt

Serves 4

1   Heat the oil in a large pan, add the onion and gently fry for 10 minutes until softened. Add the garlic, ginger, chillies and spices and fry for 2 minutes to take the raw edge off the flavour.

2   Stir in the coconut cream and fish stock, followed by the chopped tomatoes. Season, bring to the boil, then allow to bubble for 5–10 minutes until the sauce has thickened.

3   Add the prawns and simmer gently for 3 minutes until they turn pink – don't boil or they'll become tough. Check the seasoning and garnish with chopped coriander. Serve with boiled basmati rice or naan, lime wedges and chutney.

Oriental Prawn and Squid Fishcakes

Preparation Time
10 minutes
Cooking Time
about 15 minutes

- ½ onion, roughly chopped
- 1 tbsp green curry paste
- 2 tsp sesame oil
- 3 tbsp soy sauce
- a large handful of fresh coriander, plus extra to garnish
- 150g (5oz) raw peeled prawns (see Cook's Tip, page 55)
- 400g (14oz) raw squid tubes, cleaned and halved
- sunflower oil, to brush
- a few drops fish sauce
- 1 tsp soft brown sugar
- ½ red chilli, seeded and finely chopped (see Cook's Tips, page 46)
- cooked rice or seasonal vegetables to serve

NUTRITIONAL
INFORMATION
Per serving 168 calories,
7g fat (of which 1g saturates),
5g carbohydrate, 0.7g salt

Serves 4

1   Put the onion, curry paste, sesame oil, 1 tbsp soy sauce and most of the coriander into a food processor. Reserve a third each of the prawns and squid, then add the rest to the processor. Whiz to make a smooth paste, then add the remaining prawns and squid and pulse until the mixture is chunky.

2   Preheat the grill to high. Drop 16 spoonfuls of the mixture on to a non-stick baking sheet, then flatten each with a damp finger to make a rough 5cm (2in) wide patty. Brush each with a little oil and grill for 5–7 minutes on each side until they are golden and cooked through.

3   Meanwhile, in a small serving dish, stir together the remaining soy sauce and coriander, the fish sauce, sugar, chilli and 2 tsp water. Garnish the fishcakes with extra coriander leaves and serve with the dipping sauce and rice or seasonal vegetables.

Spicy Salmon Fishcakes with Zesty Vegetables

Preparation Time

Cooking Time

- ½ cucumber
- 1 each orange and yellow pepper, thinly sliced
- 12 cherry tomatoes, halved
- 6 spring onions, thinly sliced
- grated zest and juice of 1 lime, plus lime wedges to serve
- 1 tbsp sesame seeds
- 1½ tbsp clear honey
- 2 tbsp wholegrain mustard
- 4 × 125g (4oz) salmon fillets, skinned and chopped
- ½ green chilli, seeded and finely chopped (see Cook's Tips, page 46)
- 4cm (1½in) piece fresh root ginger, peeled and finely chopped
- 4 tbsp dried breadcrumbs
- 1 medium egg, beaten
- ½ tbsp sunflower oil
- a small handful of fresh mint, chopped
- salt and ground black pepper
- 4 tbsp low-fat yogurt to serve

NUTRITIONAL
INFORMATION
Per serving 457 calories,
24g fat (of which 4g saturates),
23g carbohydrate, 0.7g salt

Serves 4

1 Halve the cucumber lengthways, then scoop out the seeds with a teaspoon and discard. Cut each half into 5mm (¼in) diagonal slices and put into a bowl. Add the peppers, tomatoes and half the spring onions.

2 Mix the lime zest and juice, sesame seeds, honey and 1 tbsp mustard together in a small bowl or jug. Add a splash of water. Season, then pour over the vegetables and toss together lightly. Put to one side.

3 Put the salmon into a food processor and pulse to mince lightly. Alternatively, chop finely with a knife. Put the fish into a bowl and stir in the remaining spring onions and mustard, the chilli, ginger, breadcrumbs and egg. Season. Dampen your hands and form the mixture into eight 6.5cm (2½in) patties.

4 Heat the oil in a non-stick frying pan and fry the fishcakes for 5 minutes, turning once. Stir the mint into the vegetables and serve alongside the fishcakes, with lime wedges and yogurt seasoned with pepper.

Serves 4

Salmon and Pea Fishcakes

Preparation Time
15 minutes
Cooking Time
10–12 minutes · Serves 4

- 100g (3½oz) frozen peas
- 15 cream crackers, about 125g (4oz)
- 2 × 180g cans skinless and boneless salmon, drained
- 1 medium egg, separated
- a few drops Tabasco, to taste
- 1 tbsp freshly chopped dill
- 1 tbsp vegetable oil
- 3 tbsp mayonnaise
- 2 tbsp sweet chilli sauce
- salt and ground black pepper
- green salad to serve

NUTRITIONAL INFORMATION
Per serving: 373 calories, 22g fat (of which 4g saturates), 23g carbohydrate, 2.0g salt

1   Put the peas into a bowl, cover them with boiling water and leave for a few minutes. Meanwhile, put five of the cream crackers into a food processor and whiz until fine. Tip on to a shallow plate and put to one side for the coating. Next, whiz the remaining whole crackers until fine. Add the salmon, egg yolk, Tabasco, dill and plenty of seasoning to the processor and whiz again until combined. Drain the peas and add to the salmon mixture, then pulse briefly to combine.

2   Put the egg white into a shallow bowl and whisk lightly with a fork to break it up. Shape the fish mixture into four patties, dip each into the egg white, then coat in the reserved cracker crumbs.

3   Heat the oil in a large frying pan and cook the fishcakes for 5 minutes on each side, until golden and piping hot.

4   Meanwhile, stir the mayonnaise and sweet chilli sauce together in a small bowl. Serve the fishcakes with the dipping sauce and a green salad.

Spiced-up Salmon Noodles

Preparation Time
10 minutes
Cooking Time
10 minutes

- 1 tbsp vegetable oil
- 1 large garlic clove, crushed
- 2.5cm (1in) piece fresh root ginger, peeled and grated
- 4 × 150g (5oz) skinless and boneless salmon fillets, chopped into large pieces
- 150g (5oz) mangetouts
- a large pinch of dried chilli flakes
- 75g (3oz) tomato ketchup
- 2 tbsp soy sauce
- 2 × 300g packs bought cooked egg noodles
- 1 tbsp toasted sesame oil
- a large handful of bean sprouts
- 4 spring onions, sliced
- a large handful of fresh coriander, chopped
- salt and ground black pepper

NUTRITIONAL
INFORMATION
Per serving 455 calories,
23g fat (of which 4g saturates),
28g carbohydrate, 1.7g salt

1   Heat the vegetable oil in a large frying pan or wok over a high heat. Add the garlic and ginger and fry for 10 seconds. Add the salmon pieces and cook for 2–3 minutes until the fish turns opaque.

2   Add the mangetouts, chilli flakes, tomato ketchup, soy sauce, noodles and a splash of water and cook for 4–5 minutes. Gently stir through the sesame oil, bean sprouts and most of the spring onions and coriander. Check the seasoning.

3   Divide among four bowls, garnish with the remaining spring onions and coriander and serve immediately.

Serves 4

Serves 4

Hot-smoked Salmon and Mascarpone Pasta

Preparation Time

Cooking Time

- 400g (14oz) dried fusilli
- 5 spring onions, thinly sliced
- 2 tbsp freshly chopped dill
- 25g (1oz) pinenuts, toasted
- 175g (6oz) mascarpone
- 50ml (2fl oz) hot fish stock
- 200g (7oz) hot smoked salmon fillets, skinned and flaked
- grated zest of 1 lemon
- salt and ground black pepper

NUTRITIONAL
INFORMATION
Per serving 687 calories,
32g fat (of which 15g saturates),
76g carbohydrate, 2.5g salt

1   Bring a large pan of salted water to the boil and cook the pasta according to the pack instructions.

2   Meanwhile, mix the spring onions, dill and pinenuts together in a bowl.

3   Heat the mascarpone and stock together in a large pan. Stir until smooth, then add the salmon, lemon zest and three-quarters of the spring onion mixture. Season and heat through.

4   Drain the pasta and stir into the sauce. Garnish with the remaining spring onion mixture and serve.

Salmon with a Quick Cracker Crust

Preparation Time
10 minutes
Cooking Time
about 5 minutes

- 4 × 125g (4oz) salmon fillets, skinned
- 25g (1oz) butter, melted
- 75g (3oz) plain crackers, crushed
- 1½ tbsp fresh pesto
- 1 tbsp pinenuts, toasted
- a large handful of watercress, roughly chopped
- salt and ground black pepper
- boiled potatoes and salad to serve

NUTRITIONAL
INFORMATION
Per serving 404 calories,
26g fat (of which 7g saturates),
13g carbohydrate, 0.6g salt

Serves 4

1 Preheat the grill to medium. Line a baking sheet with greaseproof paper. Put the salmon on the paper, spacing the fillets well apart. Mix the melted butter, crackers, pesto, pinenuts, watercress and some seasoning together in a bowl and press on to the fish.

2 Grill for 3–5 minutes until the fish is cooked through and flakes easily when you push it with a knife. Serve with boiled potatoes and a salad.

Poached Salmon with Herb Sauce

Preparation Time

Cooking Time

- 1 tbsp tarragon vinegar
- 1 tbsp lemon juice
- 4 salmon fillets
- 3 lemon slices
- 1 bay leaf
- a few peppercorns
- 3 large egg yolks
- 175g (6oz) unsalted butter, melted
- 1 tbsp each freshly chopped chives and parsley
- salt and ground black pepper
- seasonal vegetables to serve

NUTRITIONAL
INFORMATION
Per serving 463 calories,
40g fat (of which 18g saturates),
1g carbohydrate, 0.2g salt

Serves 4

1   Put the vinegar and lemon juice into a small pan over a medium heat and simmer rapidly until reduced by half. Leave to cool.

2   Put the salmon into a shallow pan with the lemon, bay leaf and peppercorns and cover with cold water. Cover with a lid, bring to the boil, then remove from the heat and leave to stand for 5 minutes.

3   Meanwhile, whiz the egg yolks in a blender for a few seconds. With the blender running, slowly pour in vinegar mixture, then gradually add the melted butter. If it's too thick, add a little hot water. Transfer to a warm bowl, stir in the herbs and season to taste with salt and pepper. Serve the salmon with the sauce, pepper and seasonal vegetables.

Salmon and Bulgur Wheat Pilau

Preparation Time
5 minutes
Cooking Time
20 minutes

Serves 4

- 1 tbsp olive oil
- 1 onion, chopped
- 175g (6oz) bulgur wheat
- 450ml (¾ pint) vegetable stock
- 400g can pink salmon, drained and flaked
- 125g (4oz) spinach, roughly chopped
- 225g (8oz) frozen peas
- zest and juice of 1 lemon
- salt and ground black pepper

NUTRITIONAL INFORMATION
Per Serving 323 calories,
11g fat (of which 2g saturates),
30g carbohydrate, 1.5g salt

Try Something Different
Instead of salmon, use 200g (7oz) cooked peeled prawns and 200g (7oz) cherry tomatoes.

1   Heat the oil in a large pan, add the onion and cook until softened. Stir in the bulgur wheat to coat in the oil, then stir in the stock and bring to the boil. Cover the pan, reduce the heat and simmer for 10–15 minutes until the stock has been fully absorbed.

2   Stir in the salmon, spinach, peas and lemon juice and cook until the spinach has wilted and the salmon and peas are heated through. Season to taste with salt and pepper and sprinkle with lemon zest before serving.

Cod with Chorizo and Tomatoes

Preparation Time
10 minutes
Cooking Time
15-20 minutes

Serves 4

- 500g (1lb 2oz) baby potatoes, halved if large
- 25g (1oz) butter
- 75g (3oz) chorizo, skinned and cut into 1cm (½in) chunks
- 4 × 125g (4oz) cod or pollock fillets, skin-on
- 100ml (3½fl oz) white wine
- 200g (7oz) cherry tomatoes
- leaves from 1 fresh rosemary sprig, finely chopped
- salt and ground black pepper
- seasonal vegetables to serve

NUTRITIONAL
INFORMATION
Per serving 309 calories,
11g fat (of which 5g saturates),
24g carbohydrate, 0.5g salt

1 Cook the potatoes in a large pan of boiling salted water for 10 minutes or until tender. Drain.

2 Meanwhile, heat the butter in a large frying pan over a medium-high heat and fry the chorizo for 2 minutes or until golden. Add the cod, skin side down, and fry for 4 minutes. Carefully turn the fillets and cook for 1 minute on the other side. Lift the fish out of the pan and put on to a warm plate. Cover with foil.

3 Add the wine, tomatoes and rosemary to the pan. Bubble for 2–3 minutes until the liquid is slightly reduced and the tomatoes are starting to burst; check the seasoning. Serve the fish with the potatoes, seasonal vegetables, and spoon over the tomatoes, chorizo and pan sauce.

Pesto Cod with Butter Beans

Preparation Time
5 minutes
Cooking Time
15 minutes

- 4 cod fillets, about 150g (5oz) each
- 4 tbsp red pepper pesto
- 2 tbsp olive oil
- 2 × 400g cans butter beans, drained and rinsed
- 2 garlic cloves, crushed
- 225g (8oz) fresh spinach
- a squeeze of lemon juice
- salt and ground black pepper

NUTRITIONAL
INFORMATION
Per Serving 403 calories,
16g fat (of which 3g saturates),
24g carbohydrate, 2.5g salt

1   Preheat the grill to medium. Spread each cod fillet evenly with 1 tbsp pesto and grill for 10–15 minutes until the flesh is opaque and just cooked.

2   Meanwhile, heat the oil in a pan and add the butter beans and garlic. Cook for 10 minutes, stirring occasionally and mashing the beans lightly as they warm through. Season with salt and pepper.

3   About 2–3 minutes before serving, add the spinach to the pan and allow it to wilt. Spoon the butter beans on to four warmed plates and top with the cod and any juices from grilling. Squeeze a little lemon juice over each piece of fish and serve immediately.

Serves 4

Serves 4

Crusted Cod with Minted Pea Mash

Preparation Time
10 minutes
Cooking Time
about 15 minutes

- 50g (2oz) sun-dried tomatoes
- 2 tbsp sun-dried tomato oil (taken from the jar), plus extra to serve
- 25g (1oz) grated Parmesan
- 4 skinless cod fillets
- 500g (1lb 2oz) frozen peas
- 1 tbsp extra virgin olive oil
- a small handful of fresh mint, roughly chopped
- salt and ground black pepper

NUTRITIONAL
INFORMATION
Per serving 270 calories,
10g fat (of which 3g saturates),
12g carbohydrate, 0.3g salt

1   Preheat the oven to 200°C (180°C fan) mark 6. Put the sun-dried tomatoes, tomato oil from the jar and grated Parmesan into a blender and whiz to make a thick paste. Alternatively, bash the ingredients together using a pestle and mortar.

2   Put the cod on to a non-stick baking sheet and top each piece with a quarter of the tomato mixture. Roast in the oven for 12–15 minutes or until the fish is cooked through and flakes easily when pushed with a knife.

3   Meanwhile, bring a medium pan of water to the boil and cook the peas for 3–4 minutes until tender, then drain. Put the peas into a food processor with the extra virgin olive oil, mint and some seasoning and whiz until the mixture is the consistency of a chunky mash. Serve immediately with the cod and a drizzle of the sun-dried tomato oil.

Trout with Almonds

Preparation Time
5 minutes
Cooking Time
10–15 minutes

- 4 trout, gutted, with heads and tails intact
- 2 tbsp plain flour
- 65g (2½ oz) butter
- 50g (2oz) flaked almonds
- juice of ½ lemon, or to taste
- 1–2 tbsp freshly chopped flat-leafed parsley
- salt and ground black pepper

NUTRITIONAL
INFORMATION
Per serving 450 calories,
28g fat (of which 11g saturates),
6g carbohydrate, 1.1g salt

1   Rinse the trout and pat dry with kitchen paper. Put the flour on a plate and season with salt and pepper. Dust the fish with the seasoned flour to coat lightly. Melt 50g (2oz) of the butter in a large frying pan. Fry the trout, two at a time, for 5–7 minutes on each side, turning once, until golden on both sides and cooked.

2   Remove the fish from the pan, drain on kitchen paper and put on a warmed serving plate; keep warm. Wipe out the pan.

3   Melt the remaining butter in the pan and fry the almonds until lightly browned. Add the lemon juice and spoon over the trout. Scatter with chopped parsley and serve immediately.

Serves 4

Dover Sole with Parsley Butter

Preparation Time
5 minutes
Cooking Time
20 minutes

- 2 Dover soles, about 275g (10oz) each, gutted and descaled
- 3 tbsp plain flour
- 2 tbsp sunflower oil
- 25g (1oz) unsalted butter
- 2 tbsp freshly chopped flat-leafed parsley
- juice of ½ lemon
- salt and ground black pepper
- lemon wedges to serve

NUTRITIONAL INFORMATION
Per Serving 450 calories, 25g fat (of which 8g saturates), 16g carbohydrate, 1.5g salt

Serves 2

1 Rinse the fish under cold water, then gently pat them dry with kitchen paper. Put the flour on a large plate and season with salt and pepper. Dip the fish into the seasoned flour, to coat both sides, gently shaking off the excess.

2 Heat 1 tbsp oil in a large sauté pan or frying pan and fry one fish for 4–5 minutes on each side until golden. Transfer to a warmed plate and keep warm in a low oven. Add the remaining oil to the pan and cook the other fish in the same way; put on a plate in the oven to keep warm.

3 Add the butter to the pan and melt. Turn up the heat slightly until it turns golden, then take off the heat. Add the parsley and lemon juice, then season well. Put one fish on each warmed dinner plate and pour the parsley butter over it. Serve with lemon wedges.

Smoked Haddock Kedgeree

Preparation Time
10 minutes
Cooking Time
30 minutes

- 175g (6oz) long-grain rice
- 450g (1lb) smoked haddock fillets
- 2 medium eggs, hard-boiled and shelled
- 75g (3oz) butter
- salt and cayenne pepper
- freshly chopped flat-leafed parsley to garnish

NUTRITIONAL
INFORMATION
Per Serving: 429 calories,
20g fat (of which 11g saturates),
38g carbohydrate, 3.1g salt

Serves 4

1 Cook the rice in a pan of lightly salted fast-boiling water until tender. Drain well and rinse under cold running water.

2 Meanwhile, put the haddock into a large frying pan with just enough water to cover. Bring to simmering point, then simmer for 10–15 minutes until tender. Drain, skin and flake the fish, discarding the bones.

3 Chop one egg and slice the other into rings. Melt the butter in a pan, add the cooked rice, fish, chopped egg, salt and cayenne pepper and stir over a medium heat for 5 minutes or until hot. Pile on to a warmed serving dish and garnish with parsley and the sliced egg.

Zingy Fish One-pan

Preparation Time
10 minutes
Cooking Time
10–12 minutes

- 125g (4oz) tenderstem broccoli, halved lengthways
- 250g (9oz) fine asparagus
- 4 × 125g (4oz) skinless, boneless white fish fillets, such as haddock, pollock, cod or coley, ideally sustainably caught
- 50ml (2fl oz) white wine
- 1 orange, cut into 8 wedges
- 75g (3oz) sourdough bread, torn into pieces
- 2 tbsp olive oil
- salt and ground black pepper
- cooked rice or salad to serve

NUTRITIONAL
INFORMATION
Per Serving 228 calories,
7g fat (of which 1g saturates),
11g carbohydrate, 0.5g salt

Serves 4

1 Preheat the oven to 220°C (200°C fan) mark 7. Spread the broccoli and asparagus in an even layer in a medium roasting tin. Lay the fish fillets on top and pour over the wine. Tuck the orange wedges and bread around the fish. Drizzle over the oil and season well.

2 Cook in the oven for 10–12 minutes, or until the fish is cooked through and the vegetables are just tender (they should still have bite). Serve with rice or salad.

Grilled Fish with Rocket Pesto

Preparation Time
15 minutes
Cooking Time
3 to 5 minutes

- 50g (2oz) rocket, chopped
- grated zest and juice of ½ lemon, plus lemon wedges to serve
- ½ garlic clove, chopped
- 25g (1oz) pinenuts, toasted
- 1 small shallot, chopped
- 25ml (1fl oz) extra virgin olive oil, plus extra to grease
- 4 chunky white fish fillets, such as Alaskan pollock or Pacific cod
- salt and ground black pepper
- potato wedges to serve

NUTRITIONAL
INFORMATION
Per serving 243 calories,
12g fat (of which 1g saturates),
1g carbohydrate, 0.4g salt

Serves 4

GET AHEAD
Put the pesto into a container
with clingfilm touching the
surface and chill in the fridge
for up to three days.

1 Pulse the rocket, lemon zest and juice, garlic, pinenuts, shallot, oil and some seasoning in a food processor until smooth.

2 Preheat the grill to medium. Put the fish on to a lightly greased baking sheet and top with the rocket pesto. Grill for 3–5 minutes until the fish is opaque and flakes easily when pushed with a knife. Garnish with lemon wedges and serve with potato wedges.

Serves 4

Mediterranean Trout

Preparation Time

Cooking Time

- 4 × 175g (6oz) trout fillets
- 200g (7oz) cherry tomatoes on the vine, cut into bunches
- a large handful of fresh parsley
- 1 tbsp capers, rinsed
- ½ garlic clove
- 2 tbsp extra virgin olive oil
- 180g tub mixed chargrilled vegetables
- boiled new potatoes and a green salad to serve

NUTRITIONAL INFORMATION
Per serving 308 calories, 17g fat (of which 3g saturates), 3g carbohydrate, 2.0g salt

1   Preheat the grill to medium. Put the trout skin side up on a baking sheet and arrange the tomatoes around the fish. Grill for 3–5 minutes until the fish is nearly cooked through and the tomatoes are bursting.

2   Meanwhile, put the parsley, capers, garlic and oil in a food processor with 2 tbsp water and pulse to combine. Alternatively, bash the dressing ingredients together in a pestle and mortar.

3   Scatter the chargrilled vegetables over the fish and return to the grill for a further 2 minutes to warm through. Drizzle over the dressing and serve with new potatoes and a green salad.

Plaice with Herb and Polenta Crust

Preparation Time
15 minutes
Cooking Time
4–6 minutes

- 1 tsp finely chopped rosemary or 1 tsp finely snipped chives
- 1 tsp finely chopped thyme
- 2 garlic cloves, very finely chopped
- 50g (2oz) polenta
- finely grated zest and juice of 2 small lemons
- 2 plaice fillets, about 175g (6oz) each, skinned
- 1 large egg
- 2 tbsp olive oil
- salt and ground black pepper
- roasted tomatoes, green beans and lemon wedges to serve

NUTRITIONAL
INFORMATION
Per Serving 376 calories,
17g fat (of which 3g saturates),
19g carbohydrate, 0.6g salt

Serves 2

1   Combine the herbs, garlic and polenta on a flat plate. Add the lemon zest, salt and pepper and mix well. Wipe the plaice with kitchen paper.

2   Beat the egg in a shallow dish, dip the fish fillets in the egg and coat them with the polenta mixture, pressing it on well.

3   Heat the oil in a very large frying pan over a high heat. When hot, add the fish, reduce the heat to medium and cook for 2–3 minutes on each side, depending on the thickness of the fillets. Drain on kitchen paper. Serve with lemon juice poured over them, with roasted tomatoes, green beans and extra lemon wedges.

Tuna with Coriander Rice

Preparation Time

Cooking Time

- 250g (9oz) basmati rice
- 8 × 125g (4oz) tuna steaks
- 5cm (2in) piece fresh root ginger, peeled and grated
- 1 tbsp olive oil
- 100ml (3½fl oz) orange juice
- 300g (11oz) pak choi, roughly chopped
- a small handful of freshly chopped coriander
- ground black pepper
- lime wedges to garnish

NUTRITIONAL
INFORMATION
Per Serving 609 calories,
15g fat (of which 4g saturates),
51g carbohydrate, 0.6g salt

Cook's Tip
Basmati rice should be washed
before cooking to remove
excess starch and to give really
light, fluffy results.

Serves 4

1   Cook the rice according to the pack instructions.

2   Meanwhile, put the tuna steaks in a shallow dish. Add the ginger, oil and orange juice and season well with pepper. Turn the tuna over to coat.

3   Heat a non-stick frying pan until really hot. Add four tuna steaks and half the marinade and cook for 1–2 minutes on each side until just cooked. Repeat with the remaining tuna and marinade. Remove the fish from the pan and keep warm.

4   Add the pak choi to the frying pan and cook for 1–2 minutes until wilted. When the rice is cooked, drain and stir the coriander through it. Serve the tuna with the pak choi, rice and pan juices and garnish with lime wedges.

Classic Dressed Crab

Preparation Time
30 minutes

- 1 medium cooked crab, about 900g (2lb), cleaned (see Cook's Tip)
- 1 tbsp lemon juice
- 2 tbsp fresh white breadcrumbs
- 1 medium egg, hard-boiled
- 1 tbsp freshly chopped flat-leafed parsley
- salt and ground black pepper
- salad leaves, and brown bread and butter to serve

NUTRITIONAL
INFORMATION
Per Serving 180 calories,
8g fat (of which 1g saturates),
5g carbohydrate, 3g salt

1 Flake the white crab meat into a bowl, removing any shell or membrane, then add 1 tsp of the lemon juice and season to taste. Mix lightly with a fork.

2 Pound the brown crab meat in another bowl and work in the breadcrumbs and remaining lemon juice. Season with salt and pepper to taste.

3 Using a small spoon, put the white crab meat into the cleaned crab shell, arranging it down either side and piling it up well. Spoon the brown meat into the middle between the sections of white meat.

4 Chop the egg white; press the yolk through a sieve. To garnish the crab, spoon lines of chopped parsley, sieved egg yolk and chopped egg white along the 'joins' between the white and brown crab meat. Serve on a bed of salad leaves, with brown bread and butter.

Cook's Tips
Crab is available cooked or live, but it is better to buy a live crab and cook it at home to ensure it is perfectly fresh. Kill the crab in the same way as for lobster.
To clean the cooked crab, put the crab on a board with the belly facing up. Twist off the legs and claws. Lift off and discard the 'apron' (tail) – long and pointed in a male, short and broad in a female. Pull the body out of the shell and remove and discard the feathery gills and grey stomach sac. Use your fingers, a crab pick or a small knife to remove the white meat. Use a spoon to scrape the brown meat from the shell.

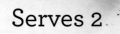

Serves 2

Crispy Crab Cakes

Preparation Time
20 minutes
Cooking Time
about 5 minutes

- 250g (9oz) white crab meat
- 4 spring onions, thinly sliced
- 7.5cm (3in) piece fresh root ginger, peeled and grated
- 4 tbsp finely chopped chives
- 1 red chilli, seeded and finely chopped (see Cook's Tips, page 46)
- 2 large eggs
- 200g (7oz) fresh white breadcrumbs
- 3 tbsp vegetable oil
- 4 tbsp good-quality mayonnaise
- finely grated zest and juice of ½ lime, plus lime wedges to serve
- salt and ground black pepper
- crisp green salad to serve

NUTRITIONAL
INFORMATION
Per serving 483 calories,
27g fat (of which 4g saturates),
40g carbohydrate, 1.9g salt

Serves 4

1   Mix the crab, spring onions, ginger, chives, chilli, eggs and breadcrumbs together in a large bowl. Season with salt and pepper and form into 16 round patties.

2   Heat the oil in a large non-stick frying pan and fry the crab cakes for 6 minutes, turning once, until golden and crisp (cook in batches, if necessary).

3   Meanwhile, mix the mayonnaise, lime zest and juice together in a bowl. Season well with salt and pepper and serve with the crab cakes, lime wedges and a crisp green salad.

Quick Crab Cakes

Preparation Time
3 minutes
Cooking Time

- 200g (7oz) fresh crabmeat
- 2 spring onions, finely chopped
- 2 red chillies, seeded and finely chopped (see Cook's Tips, page 46)
- finely grated zest of 1 lime
- 4 tbsp freshly chopped coriander
- about 40g (1½oz) wholemeal breadcrumbs
- 1 tbsp groundnut oil
- 1 tbsp plain flour
- salt and ground black pepper
- thinly sliced red chilli, seeded, to garnish
- 1 lime, cut into wedges, and salad leaves to serve

NUTRITIONAL
INFORMATION
Per Serving 124 calories,
4g fat (of which 1g saturates),
12g carbohydrate, 0.9g salt

Serves 4

Waste Not
Use leftover bread to make
breadcrumbs and freeze – a
great timesaver. You can use
them from frozen.

1   Put the crabmeat into a bowl, then mix with the spring onions, chillies, lime zest, coriander and seasoning. Add enough breadcrumbs to hold the mixture together, then form into four small patties.

2   Heat ½ tbsp oil in a pan. Dredge the patties with flour and fry on one side for 3 minutes. Add the remaining oil, then turn the patties over and fry for a further 2–3 minutes. Garnish the crab cakes with thinly sliced red chilli and serve with lime wedges to squeeze over them, and salad leaves.

Scallops with Ginger

Preparation Time
15 minutes
Cooking Time
3 minutes

- 2 tbsp vegetable oil
- 500g (1lb 2oz) shelled large scallops, cut into 5mm (¼in) slices
- 4 celery sticks, sliced diagonally
- 1 bunch of spring onions, sliced diagonally
- 25g (1oz) piece fresh root ginger, peeled and sliced
- 2 large garlic cloves, sliced
- ¼ tsp chilli powder
- 2 tbsp lemon juice
- 2 tbsp light soy sauce
- 3 tbsp freshly chopped coriander
- salt and ground black pepper

NUTRITIONAL
INFORMATION
Per Serving 197 calories,
7g fat (of which 1g saturates),
6g carbohydrate, 2g salt

1   Heat the oil in a wok or large frying pan. Add the scallops, celery, spring onions, ginger, garlic and chilli powder and stir-fry over a high heat for 2 minutes or until the vegetables are just tender.

2   Pour in the lemon juice and soy sauce, allow to bubble up, then stir in about 2 tbsp chopped coriander and season with salt and pepper. Serve immediately, sprinkled with the remaining coriander.

Serves 4

Serves 4

Mussel and Potato Stew

Preparation Time
15 minutes
Cooking Time
15 to 17 minutes

- 25g (1oz) butter
- 200g (7oz) rindless back bacon rashers, cut into strips
- 700g (1½lb) white potatoes, cut into large chunks
- 200g can sweetcorn, drained
- 1kg (2¼lb) mussels, scrubbed, rinsed and beards removed (see Cook's Tip here and on page 36)
- 150ml (¼ pint) single cream
- 1 tbsp freshly chopped flat-leafed parsley
- salt and ground black pepper

NUTRITIONAL
INFORMATION
Per Serving 470 calories,
23g fat (of which 11g saturates),
42g carbohydrate, 2.8g salt

1 Melt the butter in a large pan, add the bacon and cook, stirring, until the strips separate. Add the potatoes and 150ml (¼ pint) water and season lightly with salt and pepper. Cover with a tight-fitting lid and cook for 10 minutes or until the potatoes are almost tender.

2 Add the sweetcorn and mussels to the pan, cover and bring to the boil, then reduce the heat and simmer for 2–3 minutes until the mussels open; discard any mussels that don't open. Add the cream and chopped parsley and serve immediately.

Cook's Tip
To make sure mussels are safe to eat, check them carefully for cracks and split shells before cooking. Discard these, and any that do not close when tapped sharply. Any mussels that remain closed after cooking should also be thrown away.

Simple Smoked Haddock

Preparation Time
10 minutes
Cooking Time
about 10 minutes

- 25g (1oz) unsalted butter
- 1 tbsp olive oil
- 1 garlic clove, thinly sliced
- 4 thick smoked haddock or cod fillets,
- about 175g (6oz) each
- a small handful of freshly chopped parsley (optional)
- finely grated zest of 1 small lemon, plus lemon wedges
- to serve

NUTRITIONAL
INFORMATION
Per Serving 217 calories,
9g fat (of which 4g saturates),
1g carbohydrate, 3.4g salt

1   Heat the butter, oil and garlic in a large non-stick pan until the mixture starts to foam and sizzle. Put the fish into the pan, skin side down, and fry over a high heat for 10 minutes – this will give a golden crust underneath the fish.

2   Turn the fish over and scatter the parsley, if using, and lemon zest over it, then fry for a further 30 seconds. Put each cooked fillet on to a plate and spoon over some of the buttery juices. Serve with the lemon wedges and a green vegetable, such as romanesco broccoli.

Serves 4

Serves 4

Fish Goujons

Preparation Time

Cooking Time

- 450g (1lb) hake fillets, skinned, boned and cut into 20 even-sized pieces
- 1 medium egg, beaten
- 50g (2oz) fresh breadcrumbs
- vegetable oil for deep-frying
- Tartare Sauce to serve (see Cook's Tip)

NUTRITIONAL INFORMATION
Per Serving   267 calories,
15g fat, (of which 2g saturates),
10g carbohydrate, 0.6g salt

1 Coat the fish pieces in egg, then in the breadcrumbs.

2 Heat the oil in a deep-fat fryer to 180°C (test by frying a small cube of bread; it should brown in 40 seconds), add the fish and fry until golden. Drain on kitchen paper.

3 Serve the goujons on cocktail sticks with the sauce handed separately.

Try Something Different
Other firm fish such as haddock, coley, cod, monkfish and huss can be cooked in the same way.

Cook's Tip
Tartare Sauce Put 150ml (¼ pint) mayonnaise, 1 tsp freshly chopped tarragon or snipped chives, 2 tsp chopped capers, 2 tsp chopped gherkins, 2 tsp freshly chopped parsley and 1 tbsp lemon juice or tarragon vinegar into a bowl and mix well. Leave to stand for at least 1 hour before serving, to allow the flavours to blend. Makes 150ml (¼ pint).

Fish and Chips

Preparation Time
15 minutes
Cooking Time
12 minutes

- 4 litres (7 pints) sunflower oil for deep-frying
- 125g (4oz) self-raising flour
- ¼ tsp baking powder
- ¼ tsp salt
- 1 medium egg
- 150ml (¼ pint) sparkling mineral water
- 2 hake fillets, about 125g (4oz) each
- 450g (1lb) Desirée potatoes, peeled and cut into 1cm (½in) chips
- salt, vinegar and Lemon Mayonnaise (see Cook's Tip) to serve

NUTRITIONAL
INFORMATION
Per Serving 1186 calories,
79g fat (of which 18g saturates),
73g carbohydrate, 3.2g salt

1   Heat the oil in a deep-fryer to 190°C (test by frying a small cube of bread – it should brown in 20 seconds).

2   Whiz the flour, baking powder, salt, egg and water in a food processor or blender until combined into a batter. Remove the blade from the food processor. (Alternatively, put the ingredients into a bowl and beat everything together until smooth.) Drop one of the fish fillets into the batter to coat it.

3   Put half the chips into the deep-fryer, then add the battered fish. Fry for 6 minutes or until just cooked, then remove and drain well on kitchen paper. Keep warm if not serving immediately.

4   Drop the remaining fillet into the batter to coat, then repeat step 3 with the remaining chips. Serve with salt, vinegar and lemon mayonnaise.

Lemon Mayonnaise
Put 2 medium egg yolks, 2 tsp lemon juice, 1 tsp Dijon mustard and a pinch of sugar into a food processor. Season, then whiz briefly until pale and creamy. With the motor running, slowly pour in 300ml (½ pint) light olive oil through the feeder tube, in a steady stream, until the mayonnaise is thick. Add 1 tsp grated lemon zest and an additional 1 tbsp lemon juice and whiz briefly to combine. Store the mayonnaise in a screw-topped jar in the fridge. It will keep for up to three days.

Serves 2

Serves 4

Courgette and Anchovy Burgers

Preparation Time

Cooking Time

- 500g (1lb 2oz) courgettes
- 5 anchovy fillets in oil, finely chopped
- 50g (2oz) fresh white breadcrumbs
- 1 medium egg
- 3 tbsp chopped fresh parsley
- 1 tbsp wholegrain mustard
- plain flour to dust
- 1 tbsp sunflower oil
- 4 tbsp natural yogurt
- 4 tbsp mayonnaise
- ¼ cucumber, grated
- 1 tbsp freshly chopped mint
- salt and ground black pepper
- burger buns, toasted (optional) and salad leaves to serve

NUTRITIONAL
INFORMATION
Per serving (without bun)

253 calories, 18g fat (of which 3g saturates), 16g carbohydrate, 0.8g salt

1. Trim the courgettes, then grate them coarsely. Wrap the grated courgettes in a clean teatowel and squeeze out as much moisture as you can. Put the courgettes into a large bowl and mix through the chopped anchovies, breadcrumbs, egg, parsley, mustard and some seasoning.

2. Shape the mixture into four patties and dust them in flour. Heat the oil in a large, non-stick frying pan, add the patties and cook for 8 minutes, carefully turning them once, until golden brown and piping hot.

3. Meanwhile, mix the yogurt, mayonnaise, grated cucumber, mint and some seasoning together in a medium bowl. Serve the patties as they are, or in toasted burger buns, with the yogurt sauce and some salad leaves.

Meat-free Meals

Classic Omelette

Preparation Time
5 minutes
Cooking Time
5 minutes

- 2–3 medium eggs
- 1 tbsp milk or water
- 25g (1oz) unsalted butter
- salt and ground black pepper
- sliced or grilled tomatoes and freshly chopped flat-leafed parsley to serve

NUTRITIONAL
INFORMATION
Per Serving 449 calories,
40g fat (of which 19g saturates),
1g carbohydrate, 1g salt

Serves 1

1   Whisk the eggs in a bowl, just enough to break them down – over-beating spoils the texture of the omelette. Season with salt and pepper, and add the milk or water.

2   Heat the butter in an 18cm (7in) omelette pan or non-stick frying pan until it is foaming, but not brown. Add the eggs and stir gently with a fork or wooden spatula, drawing the mixture from the sides to the centre as it sets and letting the liquid egg in the centre run to the sides. When set, stop stirring and cook for

30 seconds or until the omelette is golden brown underneath and still creamy on top: don't overcook. If you are making a filled omelette, add the filling at this point.

3   Tilt the pan away from you slightly and use a palette knife to fold over one-third of the omelette to the centre, then fold over the opposite third. Slide the omelette out on to a warmed plate, letting it flip over so that the folded sides are underneath. Serve immediately, with tomatoes sprinkled with parsley.

Spinach and Goat's Cheese Frittata

Preparation Time
10 minutes
Cooking Time
12 minutes

- 200g (7oz) baby leeks, trimmed and chopped
- 4 spring onions, chopped
- 125g (4oz) baby leaf spinach
- 6 large eggs
- 4 tbsp milk
- freshly grated nutmeg
- 125g (4oz) soft goat's cheese, chopped
- 1 tbsp olive oil
- salt and ground black pepper
- mixed salad leaves to serve

NUTRITIONAL
INFORMATION
Per Serving 281 calories,
21g fat (of which 9g saturates),
3g carbohydrate, 0.9g salt

Serves 4

Try Something Different
Use a different cheese, such as Stilton.

1 Preheat the grill to high. Blanch the leeks in a pan of lightly salted boiling water for 2 minutes. Add the spring onions and spinach just before the end of the cooking time. Drain, rinse in cold water and dry on kitchen paper.

2 Whisk together the eggs, milk and nutmeg. Season with salt and pepper. Stir the goat's cheese into the egg mixture with the leeks, spinach and spring onions.

3 Heat the oil in a non-stick frying pan. Pour in the frittata mixture and fry gently for 4–5 minutes, then finish under the hot grill for 4–5 minutes until the top is golden and just firm. Serve with mixed salad.

Sweet Chilli Tofu Stir-fry

Preparation Time
5 minutes, plus
10 minutes marinating
Cooking Time
12 minutes

- 200g (7oz) firm tofu
- 4 tbsp sweet chilli sauce
- 2 tbsp light soy sauce
- 1 tbsp sesame seeds
- 2 tbsp toasted sesame oil
- 600g (1lb 5oz) ready-prepared mixed stir-fry vegetables, such as carrots, broccoli, mangetouts and bean sprouts
- a handful of pea shoots or young salad leaves to garnish
- rice to serve

NUTRITIONAL
INFORMATION
Per Serving 167 calories,
11g fat (of which 2g saturates),
5g carbohydrate, 1.6g salt

Serves 4

1   Drain the tofu, pat it dry and cut it into large cubes. Put the tofu in a shallow container and pour 1 tbsp sweet chilli sauce and 1 tbsp light soy sauce over it. Cover and marinate for 10 minutes.

2   Meanwhile, toast the sesame seeds in a hot wok or large frying pan until golden. Tip on to a plate.

3   Return the wok or frying pan to the heat and add 1 tbsp sesame oil. Add the marinated tofu and stir-fry for 5 minutes until golden. Remove and set aside.

4   Heat the remaining 1 tbsp oil in the pan, add the vegetables and stir-fry for 3–4 minutes until just tender. Stir in the cooked tofu.

5   Pour the remaining sweet chilli sauce and soy sauce into the pan, toss well and cook for a further minute until heated through. Sprinkle with the toasted sesame seeds and pea shoots or salad leaves, and serve immediately, with rice.

Marinated Tofu

Preparation Time
10 minutes

- finely grated zest and juice of 1 lime
- 1 spring onion, finely chopped
- ¼ red chilli, seeded and finely chopped (see Cook's Tips, page 46)
- 75g (3oz) cherry tomatoes, halved
- ½ tsp poppy seeds
- 1½ tbsp extra virgin olive oil
- 150g (5oz) silken tofu, cut into 2.5cm (1in) cubes
- a small handful of fresh coriander, roughly chopped
- salt and ground black pepper
- Easy Noodles (see page 210) to serve

NUTRITIONAL
INFORMATION
Per serving 177 calories,
15g fat (of which 2g saturates),
3g carbohydrate, 0g salt

Serves 2

1 Mix the lime zest and juice, spring onion, chilli, cherry tomatoes, poppy seeds, oil and some seasoning together in a large bowl.

2 Add the cubes of tofu and carefully toss in the marinade – if you are too rough, the tofu will crumble. Sprinkle over the chopped coriander and check the seasoning. Serve with Easy Noodles.

Serves 4

Curried Tofu Burgers

Preparation Time
20 minutes
Cooking Time
6–8 minutes

- 1 tbsp sunflower oil, plus extra to fry
- 1 large carrot, finely grated
- 1 large onion, finely grated
- 2 tsp coriander seeds, finely crushed (optional)
- 1 garlic clove, crushed
- 1 tsp curry paste
- 1 tsp tomato purée
- 225g pack firm tofu
- 25g (1oz) fresh wholemeal breadcrumbs
- 25g (1oz) mixed nuts, finely chopped
- plain flour to dust
- salt and ground black pepper
- boiled rice and green vegetables to serve

NUTRITIONAL
INFORMATION
Per Serving 253 calories,
18g fat (of which 3g saturates),
15g carbohydrate, 0.2g salt

1   Heat the oil in a large frying pan. Add the carrot and onion and fry for 3–4 minutes until the vegetables are softened, stirring all the time. Add the coriander seeds, if using, the garlic, curry paste and tomato purée. Increase the heat and cook for 2 minutes, stirring all the time.

2   Put the tofu into a bowl and mash with a potato masher. Stir in the vegetables, breadcrumbs and nuts and season with salt and pepper. Beat thoroughly until the mixture starts to stick together. With floured hands, shape the mixture into eight burgers.

3   Heat some oil in a frying pan and fry the burgers for 3–4 minutes on each side until golden brown. Alternatively, brush lightly with oil and cook under a hot grill for about 3 minutes on each side or until golden brown. Drain on kitchen paper and serve hot, with rice and green vegetables.

Veggie Bean Burgers

Preparation Time
15 minutes
Cooking Time
about 10 minutes

Serves 4

- 1 × 349g pack firm tofu
- 2½ tbsp korma curry paste
- 4 spring onions, roughly chopped
- a small handful of fresh parsley, roughly chopped
- 1 tsp paprika
- 1½ × 410g cans black eyed beans, drained and rinsed
- 50g (2oz) fresh white breadcrumbs
- ½ tbsp oil
- salt and ground black pepper
- green salald to serve

NUTRITIONAL
INFORMATION
Per serving 278 calories,
8g fat (of which 1g saturates),
34g carbohydrate, 1.8g salt

1   Preheat the grill to medium and set the grill rack 10cm (4in) away from the heat source. Put the tofu, curry paste, spring onions, parsley, paprika and lots of seasoning into a food processor and whiz until just combined, but not smooth. Add the beans and pulse briefly until they are roughly broken up. Tip the mixture into a large bowl.

2   Using your hands, add the breadcrumbs, then shapethe mixture into four equal patties (squeezing together well). Transfer the patties to a baking sheet, brush with oil and grill for 7–10 minutes until golden on top and piping hot. Serve immediately with a green salad.

Egg and Pepper Pizza

Preparation Time
15 minutes
Cooking Time
12 minutes

- 150g (5oz) red and yellow marinated peppers in oil, drained and oil put to one side
- 8 tbsp passata
- 4 small pizza bases
- 4 medium eggs
- 125g (4oz) watercress, washed and stalks removed

NUTRITIONAL INFORMATION
Per Serving 403 calories,
13g fat (of which 2g saturates),
61g carbohydrate, 1g salt

Serves 4

1 Preheat the oven to 220°C (200°C fan oven) mark 7 and preheat two large baking sheets, big enough to hold two pizzas each.

2 Chop the peppers into thin strips. Spoon 2 tbsp passata on to each pizza base and scatter strips of pepper around the edges. Make a dip in the passata in the middle of each pizza and break an egg into it. Carefully slide the pizzas on to the preheated baking sheets. Place in the oven and cook for 12 minutes until the eggs are thoroughly cooked.

3 Top the pizzas with the watercress, drizzle with a little of the reserved oil from the peppers and serve.

Chilli Bean Cake

Preparation Time
10 minutes
Cooking Time
20 minutes

- 3 tbsp olive oil
- 75g (3oz) wholemeal breadcrumbs
- 1 bunch of spring onions, finely chopped
- 1 orange pepper, seeded and chopped
- 1 small green chilli, seeded and finely chopped (see Cook's Tips, page 46)
- 1 garlic clove, crushed
- 1 tsp ground turmeric (optional)
- 400g can mixed beans, drained and rinsed
- 3 tbsp mayonnaise
- a small handful of fresh basil, chopped
- salt and ground black pepper

TO SERVE
- soured cream
- freshly chopped coriander
- lime wedges (optional)

NUTRITIONAL
INFORMATION
Per Serving 265 calories,
6g fat (of which 1g saturates),
41g carbohydrate, 2.1g salt

1   Heat 2 tbsp oil in a non-stick frying pan over a medium heat and fry the breadcrumbs until golden and beginning to crisp. Remove and put to one side.

2   Add the remaining oil to the pan and fry the spring onions until soft and golden. Add the orange pepper, chilli, garlic and turmeric, if using. Cook, stirring, for 5 minutes.

3   Tip in the beans, mayonnaise, two-thirds of the fried breadcrumbs and the basil. Season with salt and pepper, mash roughly with a fork, then press the mixture down to flatten and sprinkle with the remaining breadcrumbs. Fry the bean cake over a medium heat for 4–5 minutes until the base is golden. Remove from the heat, cut into wedges and serve with soured cream, coriander and lime wedges, if you like.

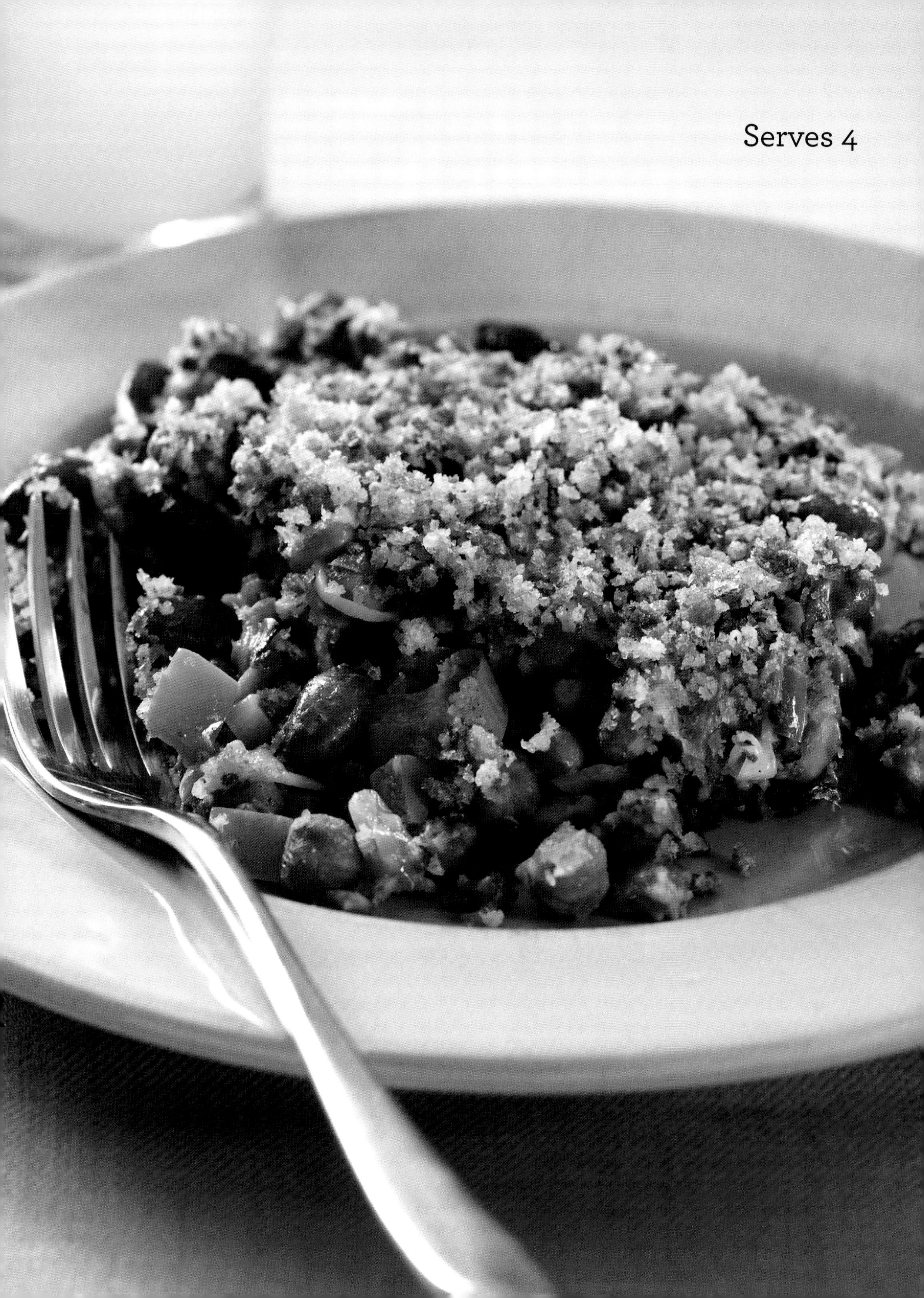

Serves 4

Easy Noodles

Preparation Time
10 minutes

- 600g (1lb 5oz) straight-to-wok rice noodles
- 1 tbsp extra virgin olive oil
- green tops from 4 spring onions, finely sliced
- salt and ground black pepper

NUTRITIONAL INFORMATION
Per serving 384 calories,
3g fat (of which 0.5g saturates),
82g carbohydrate, 0g salt

Serves 6

1 Empty the noodles into a large bowl and cover with boiling water. Leave for 5 minutes to heat through.

2 Drain and toss through the oil, spring onion tops and lots of seasoning. Serve immediately.

Aubergine and Chickpea Pilau

Preparation Time
10 minutes
Cooking Time
30 minutes, plus standing

- 4–6 tbsp olive oil
- 275g (10oz) aubergine, roughly chopped
- 225g (8oz) onions, finely chopped
- 25g (1oz) butter
- ½ tsp cumin seeds
- 175g (6oz) long-grain rice
- 600ml (1 pint) vegetable stock
- 400g can chickpeas, drained and rinsed
- 225g (8oz) baby spinach leaves
- salt and ground black pepper

NUTRITIONAL INFORMATION
Per serving 462 calories,
20g fat (of which 5g saturates),
58g carbohydrate, 0.9g salt

Serves 4

1   Heat half the oil in a large pan or flameproof casserole over a medium heat. Fry the aubergine for 4–5 minutes, in batches, until a deep golden brown. Remove from the pan with a slotted spoon and put to one side. Add the remaining oil to the pan, then add the onions and cook for 5 minutes or until golden and soft.

2   Add the butter, then stir in the cumin seeds and rice. Fry for 1–2 minutes. Pour in the stock, season with salt and pepper and bring to the boil. Reduce the heat,

then simmer, uncovered, for 10–12 minutes until most of the liquid has evaporated and the rice is tender.

3   Remove the pan from the heat. Stir in the chickpeas, spinach and reserved aubergine. Cover with a tight-fitting lid and leave to stand for 5 minutes until the spinach has wilted and the chickpeas are heated through. Adjust the seasoning to taste. Fork through the rice grains to separate and make the rice fluffy before serving.

Thai Vegetable Curry

Preparation Time
10 minutes
Cooking Time
15 minutes

- 2–3 tbsp red Thai curry paste (see Cook's Tip)
- 2.5cm (1in) piece fresh root ginger, peeled and finely chopped
- 50g (2oz) cashew nuts
- 400ml can coconut milk
- 3 carrots, cut into thin batons
- 1 broccoli head, cut into florets
- 20g (¼ oz) fresh coriander, roughly chopped
- grated zest and juice of 1 lime
- 2 large handfuls of spinach leaves
- basmati rice to serve

NUTRITIONAL INFORMATION
Per Serving 200 calories,
10g fat (of which 2g saturates),
19g carbohydrate, 0.7g salt

Serves 4

COOK'S TIP
Check the ingredients in the Thai curry paste: some contain shrimp and are therefore not suitable for vegetarians.

1   Put the curry paste into a large pan, add the ginger and cashew nuts and stir-fry over a medium heat for 2–3 minutes.

2   Add the coconut milk, cover and bring to the boil. Stir the carrots into the pan, then reduce the heat and simmer for 5 minutes. Add the broccoli florets and simmer for a further 5 minutes or until tender.

3   Stir the coriander and lime zest into the pan with the spinach. Squeeze the lime juice over the curry and serve with basmati rice.

Black-Eyed Bean Chilli

Preparation Time
10 minutes
Cooking Time
20 minutes

- 1 tbsp olive oil
- 1 onion, chopped
- 3 celery sticks, finely chopped
- 2 × 400g cans black-eyed beans, drained and rinsed
- 2 × 400g cans chopped tomatoes
- 2 or 3 splashes of Tabasco sauce
- 3 tbsp freshly chopped coriander
- 4 warmed tortillas and soured cream to serve

NUTRITIONAL
INFORMATION
Per Serving 245 calories,
5g fat (of which 1g saturates),
39g carbohydrate, 1.8g salt

Serves 4

1   Heat the oil in a frying pan. Add the onion and celery and cook for 10 minutes until softened.

2   Add the beans, tomatoes and Tabasco to the pan. Bring to the boil, then reduce the heat and simmer for 10 minutes.

3   Just before serving, stir in the coriander. Spoon the chilli on to the warm tortillas, roll up and serve with soured cream.

Weekday Suppers

Serves 1

Pork Stir-fry with Chilli and Mango

Preparation Time
5 minutes
Cooking Time
10 minutes

- 75g (3oz) medium egg noodles
- 1 tsp groundnut oil
- ½ red chilli, seeded and finely chopped (see Cook's Tips, page 46)
- 125g (4oz) pork stir-fry strips
- 1 head pak choi, roughly chopped
- 1 tbsp soy sauce
- ½ ripe mango, peeled, stoned and sliced

NUTRITIONAL INFORMATION
Per Serving 550 calories, 15g fat (of which 4g saturates), 67g carbohydrate, 3.1g salt

1 Cook the egg noodles in boiling water according to the pack instructions. Drain, then plunge into cold water and put to one side.

2 Meanwhile, put the oil into a wok or large frying pan and heat until very hot. Add the chilli and pork, and stir-fry for 3–4 minutes. Add the pak choi and soy sauce, and cook for a further 2–3 minutes. Add the mango and toss to combine.

3 Drain the noodles and add to the pan. Toss well and cook for 1–2 minutes until heated through. Serve immediately.

Cook's Tip
The smaller the chilli, the hotter it is.

Sweet and Sour Pork Stir-fry

Preparation Time
20 minutes
Cooking Time
about 10 minutes

◆ 2 tbsp vegetable oil
◆ 350g (12oz) pork fillet, cut into finger-size pieces
◆ 1 red onion, finely sliced
◆ 1 red pepper, seeded and finely sliced
◆ 2 carrots, cut into thin strips
◆ 3 tbsp sweet chilli sauce
◆ 1 tbsp white wine vinegar
◆ 220g can pineapple slices, roughly chopped, with 2 tbsp juice reserved
◆ Large handful bean sprouts
◆ ½ tbsp sesame seeds
◆ a large handful of fresh coriander, roughly chopped
◆ salt and ground black pepper
◆ cooked long-grain rice to serve

NUTRITIONAL
INFORMATION
Per Serving 282 calories,
15g fat (of which 3g saturates),
16g carbohydrate, 0.4g salt

1 Heat the oil over a high heat in a large frying pan or wok. Add the pork, onion, pepper and carrots and cook for 3–5 minutes, stirring frequently, until the meat is cooked through and the vegetables are softening.

2 Stir the sweet chilli sauce, vinegar and reserved pineapple juice into a wok or pan. Bring to the boil, then stir in the pineapple chunks and bean sprouts and heat through. Check the seasoning. Scatter over the sesame seeds and coriander and serve immediately with cooked long-grain rice.

Serves 4

Serves 4

Curry Pork Steak with Fruit Couscous

Preparation Time
10 minutes
Cooking Time
12–13 minutes

- 4 × 150g (5oz) pork shoulder steaks
- 2 tbsp medium-hot curry paste
- 150g (5oz) couscous
- 400g can chickpeas, drained and rinsed
- 250ml (9fl oz) boiling chicken stock
- 75g (3oz) sultanas
- zest and juice of 1 lime
- a large handful of fresh parsley, chopped
- 4 tsp aubergine (brinjal) pickle
- salt and ground black pepper
- green salad to serve

NUTRITIONAL INFORMATION
Per Serving 592 calories,
31g fat (of which 8g saturates),
46g carbohydrate, 1.4g salt

1 Preheat the grill to high. Put the pork steaks on a board, cover with clingfilm and flatten slightly with a rolling pin. Transfer to a bowl, add the curry paste and plenty of seasoning and stir to coat. Arrange the steaks on a non-stick baking tray, then grill for 12–13 minutes, turning once, until golden and cooked through.

2 Meanwhile, put the couscous and chickpeas in a large bowl and pour over the boiling stock. Cover with clingfilm and put to one side for 5 minutes, then use a fork to fluff up. Stir in the sultanas, lime zest and juice and most of the parsley.

3 When the pork is cooked through, spoon 1 tsp aubergine pickle on top of each steak, then garnish with the remaining parsley. Serve the pork with the couscous and a green salad.

Flash in the Pan Pork

Preparation Time
5 minutes
Cooking Time
15 minutes

- 700g (1½lb) new potatoes, scrubbed, halved if large
- 175g (6oz) runner beans, sliced
- a little sunflower or olive oil
- 4 pork escalopes
- 150ml (¼ pint) hot chicken stock
- 150ml (¼ pint) apple cider
- 2 tbsp wholegrain mustard
150g (5oz) Greek yogurt
- 4 fresh tarragon stems, leaves only
- a squeeze of lemon juice
- salt

NUTRITIONAL INFORMATION
Per Serving 346 calories,
12g fat (of which 4g saturates),
32g carbohydrate, 0.6g salt

Serves 4

1 Cook the new potatoes in a large pan of boiling salted water for 10 minutes. Add the beans and cook for a further 5 minutes or until tender. Drain.

2 Meanwhile, heat the oil in a large non-stick frying pan over a medium heat, and cook the pork for 3 minutes on each side until browned. Remove from the pan and keep warm. Add the stock, cider and mustard to the pan, and increase the heat to reduce the liquid by half.

3 Just before serving, reduce the heat and add the yogurt, tarragon leaves and lemon juice. Put the pork back in the pan to coat with the sauce and warm through. Serve with the potatoes and beans.

Cumin-spiced Gammon

Preparation Time
10 minutes
Cooking Time
10 minutes

- large pinch each of ground cumin and paprika
- 2 tbsp olive oil
- 2 tsp light muscovado sugar
- 8 thin smoked gammon steaks, about 125g (4oz) each
- 2 large ripe papayas
- zest and juice of 2 limes
- ½ red chilli, seeded and finely chopped (see Cook's Tips, page 46)
- 20g (¾oz) fresh mint, finely chopped
- steamed green beans to serve

NUTRITIONAL INFORMATION
Per Serving 492 calories,
18g fat (of which 5g saturates),
3g carbohydrate, 13.8g salt

Serves 4

1   Preheat the grill. In a small bowl, mix together the cumin, paprika, oil and half the sugar. Put the gammon on to a non-stick baking sheet, then brush the spiced oil over each side.

2   Grill the gammon for about 5 minutes on each side, basting once or twice with the juices.

3   Meanwhile, cut each papaya in half, then seed and peel. Roughly chop half the flesh and put into a bowl. Purée the remaining fruit with the lime juice. Add to the bowl with the lime zest, chilli, mint and remaining sugar. Spoon the mixture on top of the gammon and serve with green beans.

Pork Escalopes and Apple Slaw

Preparation Time
20 minutes
Cooking Time
about 5 minutes

- 200g (7oz) 0% fat Greek yogurt
- juice of 1 lemon
- 1 tsp wholegrain mustard
- 2 eating apples (skin on), cut into matchsticks
- ½ small red cabbage, finely shredded
- a small handful of fresh parsley, chopped
- 75g (3oz) Rice Krispies
- 25g (1oz) plain flour
- 2 medium eggs, beaten
- 4 pork escalopes
- 2 tbsp sunflower oil
- salt and ground black pepper
- boiled new potatoes to serve

NUTRITIONAL INFORMATION
Per Serving 365 calories,
13g fat (of which 3g saturates),
34g carbohydrate, 0.7g salt

Get Ahead
Complete the recipe to the end of step 2 up to one day in advance. Cover and chill the slaw and coated escalopes. Complete the recipe to serve.

Serves 4

1 Put the yogurt, lemon juice and mustard into a large serving bowl and mix together. Stir in the apple matchsticks, cabbage and parsley. Check the seasoning and put to one side.

2 Whiz the Rice Krispies in a food processor until finely crushed. Tip on to a lipped plate. Put the flour and eggs on two separate lipped plates.

3 Dip each escalope into the flour to coat, tapping off any excess, then dip into the beaten eggs, followed by the cereal crumbs. Finish by dipping each escalope once more into the eggs before coating with a final layer of cereal.

4 Heat the oil in a large, non-stick frying pan over a medium heat. Add the escalopes and fry for 5 minutes, turning once, until golden and cooked through. Serve with the apple slaw and boiled new potatoes.

Italian Sausage Stew

Preparation Time
10 minutes
Cooking Time
15 minutes

- 25g (1oz) dried porcini mushrooms
- 300g (11oz) whole rustic Italian salami sausages, such as salami Milano
- 2 tbsp olive oil
- 1 onion, sliced
- 2 garlic cloves, chopped
- 1 small red chilli, seeded and chopped (see Cook's Tips, page 46)
- 1 fresh rosemary sprig
- 400g can chopped tomatoes
- 200ml (7fl oz) red wine
- ground black pepper
- freshly chopped flat-leafed parsley to garnish
- tagliatelle or fettucine to serve

NUTRITIONAL INFORMATION
Per Serving 443 calories,
35g fat (of which 12g saturates),
6g carbohydrate, 3.4g salt

Serves 4

1 Put the dried mushrooms in a small bowl, pour on 100ml (3½fl oz) boiling water and leave to soak for 20 minutes, or soften in the microwave on full power for 3½ minutes and leave to cool. Cut the salami into 1cm (½in) slices and put to one side.

2 Heat the oil in a pan, add the onion, garlic and chilli and fry gently for 5 minutes. Meanwhile, strip the leaves from the rosemary sprig and add them to the pan, stirring. Add the salami and fry for 2 minutes on each side or until browned. Drain and chop the mushrooms and add them to the pan. Stir in the chopped tomatoes and red wine, then season with pepper. Simmer, uncovered, for 5 minutes. Sprinkle with parsley and serve with tagliatelle or fettucine.

Satay Pork Curry

Preparation Time
15 minutes
Cooking Time
about 15 minutes

- ½ tbsp vegetable oil
- ½ tbsp ground coriander
- 1 garlic clove, finely chopped
- 500g (1lb 2oz) pork fillet, cut into 1cm (½in) rounds
- 150g (5oz) mangetouts
- 200g (7oz) baby sweetcorn, chopped
- 2 tbsp medium curry paste
- 2 tbsp crunchy peanut butter
- 1 tbsp light soft brown sugar
- 100ml (3½fl oz) full-fat coconut milk
- 100ml (3½fl oz) vegetable or chicken stock
- juice of 1 lemon
- a large handful of fresh coriander
- egg noodles to serve

NUTRITIONAL INFORMATION
Per Serving (without noodles)
369 calories, 22g fat
(of which 8g saturates),
11g carbohydrate, 0.6g salt

1   Heat the oil in a large frying pan over a medium heat. Add the ground coriander and garlic and fry for 30 seconds. Add the pork and fry for a further 5 minutes until golden, turning occasionally. Add the mangetouts and sweetcorn to the pan and fry for 3 minutes. Lift out the pork and vegetables and put to one side.

2   Add the curry paste to the empty pork pan and stir in the peanut butter and sugar. Cook for 1 minute, then stir in the coconut milk and stock until smooth. Bring to the boil, then reduce the heat and simmer for 3 minutes until the sauce thickens.

3   Return the pork and vegetables to the pan and simmer for 3–5 minutes until the vegetables are tender and the meat is cooked through. Stir in the lemon juice and coriander and serve with egg noodles.

Serves 4

Jerk Chicken

Preparation Time
10 minutes
Cooking Time
about 15 minutes

- 1 tbsp fresh thyme leaves
- 2.5cm (1in) piece fresh root ginger, peeled and grated
- 1 tsp ground allspice
- 1 tbsp white wine vinegar
- 1 tsp soy sauce
- 1 garlic clove, crushed
- 2 green chillies, seeded and finely chopped (see Cook's Tips, page 46)
- 3 tbsp vegetable oil
- 8 chicken pieces, such as thighs and drumsticks
- boiled basmati rice and a green salad or seasonal vegetables to serve

NUTRITIONAL INFORMATION
Per Serving 327 calories,
26g fat (of which 6g saturates),
1g carbohydrate, 0.1g salt

Serves 4

1. Preheat the grill to medium and set the grill rack about 15cm (6in) from heat. Use a blender or a pestle and mortar to combine the thyme, ginger, allspice, vinegar, soy sauce, garlic, chillies and oil until smooth.

2 Put the chicken pieces on to a foil-lined baking sheet, then pour over the jerk marinade and rub into the chicken. Grill for 12–15 minutes until golden and cooked through. Serve with boiled basmati rice, and a green salad or seasonal vegetables.

Chicken Laksa

Preparation Time
10 minutes
Cooking Time
about 10 minutes

- 1 tbsp olive oil
- 4 × 125g (4oz) chicken breasts, diced
- 1–3 tbsp green Thai curry paste, to taste
- 2 sweet potatoes (about 350g/12oz), diced
- 400ml can coconut milk
- 400ml (¾ pint) hot water
- a large handful of fresh coriander, roughly chopped
- salt and ground black pepper

NUTRITIONAL INFORMATION
Per Serving 502 calories,
26g fat (of which 17g saturates),
27g carbohydrate, 0.4g salt

Serves 4

COOK'S TIP
To turn this recipe into a more substantial meal, stir in some noodles with the coconut milk, then complete the recipe to serve.

1   Heat the oil in a large pan over a high heat. Add the chicken breasts, Thai curry to taste and the sweet potatoes and fry for 5 minutes, stirring frequently. Pour in the coconut milk and 400ml (¾ pint) hot water. Bring to the boil, then reduce the heat and simmer for 5 minutes or until the chicken and potatoes are cooked through.

2   Stir through the coriander and check the seasoning. Spoon into warmed bowls and serve immediately.

Speedy Chicken Pilaf

Preparation Time
5 minutes
Cooking Time
about 20 minutes

- 1 tbsp oil
- 1 onion, finely sliced
- 1 tbsp balti curry paste
- 6 skinless chicken thigh fillets, cut into finger-size strips
- 2 × 250g pouches cooked rice
- 150g (5oz) peas
- 100g (3½oz) spinach
- 2 tbsp mango chutney, plus extra to serve
- flaked almonds (optional)
- salt and ground black pepper

NUTRITIONAL INFORMATION
Per Serving (without almonds)
505 calories, 16g fat
(of which 4g saturates),
54g carbohydrate, 0.6g salt

Serves 4

1 Heat the oil in a large pan over a medium heat. Add the onion and fry for 5 minutes until beginning to soften. Stir in the curry paste and cook for 1 minute, then add the chicken and fry for 8 minutes until cooked through. Add a splash of water if the pan looks dry.

2 Stir in the rice, peas and 100ml (3½fl oz) water, then cook for 3 minutes until the rice is fully tender. Stir through the spinach and chutney, then check the seasoning. Scatter with almonds (if using) and serve with some extra mango chutney on the side.

Mexican Chicken with Pepper Salsa

Preparation Time
15 minutes
Cooking Time
about 15 minutes

Serves 4

- 4 × 125g (4oz) chicken breasts, skinless
- 3 tbsp tomato purée
- 1½ tsp smoked paprika
- ½ tsp sugar
- juice of 1 lime
- ½ tsp oil
- 290g jar roasted red peppers in water, drained and chopped
- 2 tomatoes, finely chopped
- 1 red onion, finely chopped
- a large handful of fresh coriander, chopped
- salt and ground black pepper
- lime wedges and cooked rice or wholemeal tortillas to serve

NUTRITIONAL INFORMATION
Per Serving 237 calories,
5g fat (of which 1g saturates),
10g carbohydrate, 0.3g salt

1 Put the chicken breasts between two sheets of clingfilm and flatten slightly with a rolling pin. Stir the purée, paprika, sugar, lime juice, oil and some seasoning together in a large bowl. Add the chicken and coat.

2 Heat a griddle pan and cook the chicken for 12–15 minutes, turning once, until cooked through. In a separate bowl, stir the peppers, tomatoes, onion and coriander together. Serve the chicken and salsa with lime wedges and cooked rice or wholemeal tortillas.

Spiced Tikka Kebabs

Preparation Time
10 minutes
Cooking Time
20 minutes

- ◆ 2 tbsp tikka paste
- ◆ 150g (5oz) natural yogurt
- ◆ juice of ½ lime
- ◆ 4 spring onions, chopped
- ◆ 350g (12oz) skinless chicken,
- ◆ cut into bite-sized pieces
- ◆ lime wedges to serve

**NUTRITIONAL
INFORMATION**
Per Serving 150 calories,
5g fat (of which 1g saturates),
4g carbohydrate, 0.3g salt

1 Preheat the grill. Put the tikka paste, yogurt, lime juice and chopped spring onions into a large bowl. Add the chicken and toss well. Thread the chicken on to skewers.

2 Grill for 8–10 minutes on each side or until cooked through, turning and basting with the paste. Serve with lime wedges to squeeze over the kebabs.

Cook's Tip
Serve with rocket salad put 75g (3oz) rocket in a large bowl. Add ¼ chopped avocado, a handful of halved cherry tomatoes, ½ chopped cucumber and the juice of 1 lime. Season with salt and pepper and mix together.

Mediterranean Chicken

Preparation Time
5 minutes
Cooking Time
20 minutes

- 1 red pepper, seeded and chopped
- 2 tbsp capers
- 2 tbsp freshly chopped rosemary
- 2 tbsp olive oil
- 4 skinless chicken breasts, about 125g (4oz) each
- salt and ground black pepper
- cooked rice or new potatoes to serve

NUTRITIONAL INFORMATION
Per Serving 223 calories,
7g fat (of which 1g saturates),
3g carbohydrate, 0.2g salt

Serves 4

Try Something Different
Use chopped black olives instead of the capers.

1 Preheat the oven to 200°C (180°C fan oven) mark 6. Put the red pepper into a medium bowl with the capers, rosemary and oil. Season with salt and pepper and mix well.

2 Put the chicken breasts into an ovenproof dish and spoon the pepper mixture over the top. Cook in the oven for 15–20 minutes until the chicken is cooked through and the topping is hot. Serve with rice or new potatoes.

Cheat's Oven Kievs

Preparation Time
15 minutes
Cooking Time
25 minutes

- 4 × 125g (4oz) skinless chicken breasts
- 50g (2oz) garlic and herb Boursin
- 75g (3oz) fresh white breadcrumbs
- 1 medium egg
- 25g (1oz) butter, melted
- a small handful of fresh curly parsley, finely chopped
- salt and ground black pepper
- green salad and boiled new potatoes to serve

NUTRITIONAL INFORMATION
Per Serving   373 calories, 16g fat (of which 8g saturates), 15g carbohydrate, 0.8g salt

Serves 4

Freeze Ahead
Complete the recipe to the end of step 2. Leaving the chicken on the sheet, wrap well in clingfilm and freeze for up to one month. To serve, allow the chicken to defrost on the sheet in the fridge overnight, then unwrap the clingfilm and complete the recipe.

1 Preheat the oven to 200°C (180°C fan) mark 6. Cut a slit in the side of a chicken breast and use your finger to work it into a pocket. Repeat with the remaining breasts. Stuff each pocket with a quarter of the Boursin, seal with a cocktail stick and arrange the stuffed breasts on a non-stick baking sheet.

2 In a medium bowl, mix together the remaining ingredients and some seasoning. Pat a quarter of the bread mixture on top of each chicken breast.

3 Cook for 25 minutes or until the breasts are cooked through. Remove the cocktail sticks and serve with a green salad and boiled new potatoes.

Basil and Lemon Chicken

Preparation Time
15 minutes, plus minimum
15 minutes marinating

- grated zest of 1 lemon, plus
  4 tbsp lemon juice
- 1 tsp caster sugar
- 1 tsp Dijon mustard
- 175ml (6fl oz) lemon-infused
  oil
- 4 tbsp freshly chopped basil
- 2 x 210g packs roast chicken
- 250g (9oz) baby leaf spinach
- 55g pack crisp bacon, broken
  into small pieces
- salt and ground black pepper

**NUTRITIONAL
INFORMATION**
Per Serving 331 calories,
25g fat (of which 5g saturates),
2g carbohydrate, 1.3g salt

Serves 4

1 Put the lemon zest and juice, sugar, mustard and oil in a small bowl. Season with salt and pepper. Whisk together until thoroughly combined, then add the basil.

2 Remove any bones from the roast chicken, leave the skin attached and slice into five or six pieces. Arrange the sliced chicken in a dish and pour the dressing over, then cover and leave to marinate for at least 15 minutes.

3 Just before serving, lift the chicken from the dressing and put to one side.

4 Put the spinach in a large bowl, pour the dressing over and toss together. Arrange the chicken on top of the spinach, and sprinkle with the bacon. Serve immediately.

Chicken with Black-Eye Beans and Greens

Preparation Time
5 minutes
Cooking Time
15 minutes

- 2 tsp Jamaican jerk seasoning
- 4 chicken breasts
- 1kg (2¼lb) spring greens or cabbage, core removed and shredded
- 2 × 300g cans black-eye beans, drained and rinsed
- 8 tbsp olive oil
- juice of 1¼ lemons
- salt and ground black pepper

NUTRITIONAL INFORMATION
Per Serving 491 calories,
26g fat (of which 4g saturates),
31g carbohydrate, 1.5g salt

Serves 4

1 Preheat the grill. Rub the jerk seasoning into the chicken breasts, and sprinkle with salt. Cook under the grill for 15 minutes or until done, turning from time to time.

2 Cook the spring greens or cabbage in salted boiling water until just tender – bringing the water back to the boil after adding the greens is usually enough to cook them. Drain and put back in the pan.

3 Add the beans and olive oil to the greens, and season well with salt and pepper. Heat through and add the juice of 1 lemon.

4 To serve, slice the chicken and place on the bean mixture, then drizzle over the remaining lemon juice and serve.

Serves 4

Turkey Breast with Fiery Honey Sauce

Preparation Time
15 minutes
Cooking Time
about 15 minutes

- ½ tbsp olive oil
- 4 turkey breast steaks, total about 500g (1lb 2oz)
- 1 tbsp Worcestershire sauce
- ½–1 red chilli, to taste, seeded and finely chopped (see Cook's Tips, page 46)
- 1½ tbsp runny honey
- 100ml (3½fl oz) chicken stock
- 4 spring onions, finely sliced
- salt and ground black pepper
- seasonal vegetables, cooked noodles or salad to serve

NUTRITIONAL
INFORMATION
Per Serving 201 calories,
2g fat (of which 1g saturates),
7g carbohydrate, 0.5g salt

1   Heat the oil in a large frying pan over a medium-high heat and cook the turkey steaks for 8–10 minutes, turning once, until cooked through. Put to one side on a board, cover well with foil to keep warm and leave to rest while you prepare the sauce.

2   Return the pan to the heat and add the Worcestershire sauce, chilli, honey, stock, spring onions and some seasoning. Heat through and leave to bubble for 2 minutes until slightly thickened.

3   Serve the turkey and sauce with some seasonal vegetables, cooked noodles or salad.

Zesty Turkey One-Pan

Preparation Time
10 minutes
Cooking Time
about 10 minutes

- ½ tbsp olive oil
- 4 turkey breast steaks, total about 500g (1lb 2oz)
- 350ml (12fl oz) chicken stock
- grated zest and juice of 2 lemons
- 25g (1oz) capers, rinsed and chopped
- 4 tomatoes, roughly chopped
- a large handful of fresh curly parsley, roughly chopped
- salt and ground black pepper
- cooked rice, seasonal vegetables or salad to serve

NUTRITIONAL INFORMATION
Per Serving 203 calories,
4g fat (of which 1g saturates),
3g carbohydrate, 1.0g salt

1 Heat the oil in a large frying pan over a high heat and fry the turkey steaks for 2 minutes, turning once, to brown the steaks. Add the stock, lemon zest and juice, the capers, tomatoes and some seasoning. Simmer for 8 minutes until the turkey is cooked through.

2 Add the parsley and check the seasoning. Serve with cooked rice, seasonal vegetables or salad.

Cook's Tip
This zingy supper would be wonderful made with chicken, your favourite white fish fillets or even prawns.

Serves 4

Serves 4

Sweet Chilli Beef Stir-fry

Preparation Time
10 minutes
Cooking Time
15 minutes

- 1 tsp chilli oil
- 1 tbsp soy sauce
- 1 tbsp clear honey
- 1 garlic clove, crushed
- 1 large red chilli, halved, seeded and chopped (see Cook's Tips, page 46)
- 400g (14oz) lean beef, cut into strips
- 1 tsp sunflower oil
- 1 broccoli head, sliced into small florets
- 200g (7oz) mangetouts, halved
- 1 red pepper, halved, seeded and cut into strips

NUTRITIONAL INFORMATION
Per Serving 273 calories,
13g fat (of which 5g saturates),
8g carbohydrate, 0.2g salt

1 Put the chilli oil in a medium-sized shallow bowl. Add the soy sauce, honey, garlic and chilli, and stir well. Add the strips of beef and toss in the marinade.

2 Heat the sunflower oil in a wok over a high heat until it is very hot. Cook the strips of beef in two batches, then remove them from the pan and put to one side and keep warm. Wipe the pan with kitchen paper to remove any residue.

3 Add the broccoli, mangetouts, red pepper and 2 tbsp water. Stir fry for 5–6 minutes until starting to soften. Return the beef to the pan to heat through.

Try Something Different
Other vegetables are just as good try pak choi, baby sweetcorn, courgettes or carrots cut into thin strips.

Steak Salad with Warm Chilli Dressing

Preparation Time
15 minutes
Cooking Time
about 15 minutes

- 500g (1lb 2oz) baby new potatoes, halved if large
- 1 tbsp sunflower oil
- 3 tbsp each soy and sweet chilli sauce
- 1 tsp runny honey
- juice of 1 lime, plus lime wedges to serve
- 2 × 250g (9oz) sirloin steaks
- 3 spring onions, thinly sliced
- 10 radishes, sliced
- 25g pack basil leaves, roughly torn
- a few large handfuls of mixed leaves

NUTRITIONAL INFORMATION
Per Serving 403 calories,
20g fat (of which 8g saturates),
26g carbohydrate, 1.0g salt

1 Cook the potatoes in a pan of boiling water until tender. Drain and put to one side.

2 Meanwhile, in a large shallow dish, mix together half the oil, the soy and sweet chilli sauces, honey and half the lime juice. Add the steaks and turn to coat.

3 Heat the remaining oil in a frying pan until hot. Lift the steaks out of the marinade, reserving the liquid, and fry for 2 minutes on each side for rare. Cook for a little longer if you prefer your meat less pink. Remove from the pan and put on a board. Cover with foil and leave to rest for 5 minutes.

4 Meanwhile, put the pan back over the heat and add the reserved marinade and remaining lime juice. Bring to a simmer and bubble for 1–2 minutes to thicken slightly. Thinly slice steaks, discarding excess fat. Put into a serving bowl with the potatoes, spring onions, radishes, basil and mixed leaves. Drizzle over the pan dressing and serve immediately with lime wedges on the side.

Get Ahead
Marinate the steak in advance, then cover and refrigerate for up to one day. Bring to room temperature before cooking.

Serves 4

Fruity Beef Stir-fry

Preparation Time
20 minutes
Cooking Time
about 5 minutes

- ½ tbsp vegetable oil
- 400g (14oz) sirloin steak, excess fat trimmed, cut into strips
- 1 each red and green pepper, seeded and finely sliced
- 5cm (2in) piece fresh root ginger, peeled and cut into matchsticks
- 2 tbsp soy sauce
- 1 ripe mango, peeled, stoned and cut into 1cm (½in) chunks
- a large handful of bean sprouts
- 1 tsp toasted sesame oil
- 1 tsp sesame seeds
- a small handful of fresh coriander, to garnish
- salt and ground black pepper
- lime wedges and noodles to serve

NUTRITIONAL INFORMATION
Per Serving 212 calories, 8g fat (of which 3g saturates), 10g carbohydrate, 0.2g salt

Serves 4

Cook's Tip
Have all your ingredients prepared and to hand before you start stir-frying to ensure everything is cooked to perfection!

1 Heat the vegetable oil in a large wok or frying pan over a high heat. Add the steak strips and brown all over for 1 minute. Add the peppers and stir-fry for 3 minutes.

2 Stir in the ginger, soy sauce and a splash of water, followed by the mango and bean sprouts. Heat through, then check the seasoning. Drizzle over the toasted sesame oil, sprinkle over the sesame seeds and garnish with coriander. Serve with lime wedges and noodles.

Steak and Asparagus Stir-fry

Preparation Time
10 minutes
Cooking Time
about 10 minutes

Serves 4

- 1 × 225g (8oz) rump steak, trimmed and sliced
- 2 tbsp honey
- 2 tbsp teriyaki sauce
- 1 tbsp sesame oil
- 150g (5oz) each tenderstem broccoli and asparagus, cut into 5cm (2in) lengths
- 75g (3oz) water chestnuts
- 1 tbsp sesame seeds
- salt and ground black pepper
- cooked brown rice to serve

NUTRITIONAL INFORMATION

Per Serving 188 calories, 7g fat (of which 2g saturates), 15g carbohydrate, 0.1g salt

1 Put the beef, honey, teriyaki sauce and sesame oil into a bowl. Stir and leave to marinate for 5 minutes.

2 Heat a wok over a high heat. Lift the beef out of the marinade (reserving the mixture) and stir-fry for 3 minutes until caramelised and cooked to medium (cook for longer or shorter, if you prefer). Empty the beef into a clean bowl and put to one side.

3 Return the wok to the heat, and add the broccoli, asparagus and a splash of water. Fry for 3 minutes until the vegetables are just tender. Stir in the marinade, water chestnuts and beef and heat for 30 seconds. Check the seasoning. Sprinkle over the sesame seeds and serve immediately with cooked brown rice.

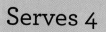
Serves 4

Harissa Lamb with Bulgur Wheat

Preparation Time
20 minutes
Cooking Time
about 10 minutes

- 200g (7oz) bulgur wheat
- ½ tsp each ground cinnamon and cumin
- 4 tomatoes, quartered and seeded
- 75g (3oz) dried apricots, finely chopped
- 3 tbsp extra virgin olive oil
- finely grated zest and juice of ½ orange
- 2 tbsp finely chopped fresh oregano
- 12 lamb cutlets, trimmed of excess fat
- ¼ tsp harissa paste
- salt and ground black pepper

NUTRITIONAL INFORMATION
Per Serving 699 calories,
34g fat (of which 12g saturates),
54g carbohydrate, 0.2g salt

1 Toast the bulgur wheat and spices in a large frying pan for 2 minutes until lightly golden. Empty into a large bowl, then pour over enough boiling water to just cover the bulgur. Cover with clingfilm and leave for 10 minutes.

2 Meanwhile, finely chop the tomatoes and tip into a large serving bowl with the apricots, 2 tbsp of the oil, the orange zest and juice, and oregano. Season well with salt and pepper.

3 Brush both sides of the lamb cutlets with harissa. Heat the remaining oil in the frying pan used to toast the bulgur wheat and fry the cutlets for 6 minutes, turning once. Cook for 1 minute longer per side for well-done meat. Put the cutlets to one side to rest for 1 minute.

4 Use a fork to stir the bulgur wheat into the tomato mixture. Check the seasoning and serve with the cutlets.

Cooking for Friends

Serves 6

Thai Green Curry

Preparation Time
10 minutes
Cooking Time
15 minutes

- 2 tsp vegetable oil
- 1 green chilli, seeded and finely chopped (see Cook's Tips, page 46)
- 4cm (1½in) piece fresh root ginger, peeled and finely grated
- 1 lemongrass stalk, trimmed and cut into three pieces
- 225g (8oz) brown-cap or oyster mushrooms
- 1 tbsp Thai green curry paste
- 300ml (½ pint) coconut milk
- 150ml (¼ pint) chicken stock
- 1 tbsp Thai fish sauce
- 1 tsp light soy sauce
- 350g (12oz) boneless, skinless chicken breasts, cut into bite-size pieces
- 350g (12oz) cooked peeled large prawns
- fresh coriander sprigs to garnish
- Thai fragrant rice to serve

NUTRITIONAL INFORMATION
Per Serving 132 calories,
2g fat (of which 0g saturates),
4g carbohydrate, 1.4g salt

1   Heat the oil in a wok or large frying pan, add the chilli, ginger, lemongrass and mushrooms and stir-fry for about 3 minutes or until the mushrooms begin to turn golden. Add the curry paste and fry for a further 1 minute.

2   Pour in the coconut milk, stock, fish sauce and soy sauce and bring to the boil. Stir in the chicken, then reduce the heat and simmer for about 8 minutes or until the chicken is cooked.

3   Add the prawns and cook for a further 1 minute. Garnish with coriander sprigs and serve immediately, with Thai fragrant rice.

Easy Thai Red Curry

Preparation Time
5 minutes
Cooking Time
20 minutes

- 1 tbsp vegetable oil
- 3 tbsp Thai red curry paste
- 4 skinless chicken breasts, about 600g (1lb 5oz) total weight, sliced
- 400ml can coconut milk
- 300ml (½ pint) hot chicken or vegetable stock
- juice of 1 lime, plus lime halves to serve
- 200g pack mixed baby sweetcorn and mangetouts
- 2 tbsp freshly chopped coriander, plus sprigs to garnish
- rice or rice noodles to serve

NUTRITIONAL INFORMATION
Per Serving 248 calories, 8g fat (of which 1g saturates), 16g carbohydrate, 1g salt

1 Heat the oil in a wok or large frying pan over a low heat. Add the curry paste and cook for 2 minutes or until fragrant.

2 Add the sliced chicken and fry gently for about 10 minutes or until the chicken is browned.

3 Add the coconut milk, hot stock, lime juice and baby sweetcorn to the pan and bring to the boil. Add the mangetouts, then reduce the heat and simmer for 4–5 minutes until the chicken is cooked. Stir in the chopped coriander, garnish with coriander sprigs and serve immediately with rice or noodles, and lime halves to squeeze over.

Serves 4

Serves 4

Stuffed Chicken Breasts

Preparation Time
10 minutes
Cooking Time
about 12–15 minutes

- ◆ 4 skinless chicken breasts
- ◆ 4tbsp red onion marmalade
- ◆ 75g (3oz) soft goat's cheese
- ◆ 1 tbsp vegetable oil
- ◆ seasonal vegetables or a
  green salad to serve

**NUTRITIONAL
INFORMATION**
Per Serving 488 calories,
14g fat (of which 5g saturates),
23g carbohydrate, 0.5g salt

1 Put a chicken breast in front of you on a board. Slice in half horizontally through the side, but don't cut all the way through. Open the chicken breast out like a book, then flatten by hitting with a rolling pin. Repeat with the remaining breasts.

2 Spread a quarter of the marmalade over one side of each breast, leaving a slight border, then crumble over a quarter of the cheese. Fold in half again and seal with cocktail sticks. Brush well with oil.

3 Heat a griddle or frying pan and cook the chicken breasts for 12–15 minutes, turning once, until cooked through (check carefully, as the marmalade can stain the chicken pink, making it look uncooked). Serve with seasonal vegetables or a green salad.

Chicken Fajitas

Preparation Time
1 minutes
Cooking Time
about 5 minutes

- 4 large flour tortilla wraps
- 2 tsp oil
- 1 garlic clove, crushed
- ½–1 tsp smoked paprika, to taste
- 2 tbsp tomato purée
- 1 tsp runny honey
- 4 cooked skinless chicken breasts, cut into finger-sized strips
- 125g (4oz) roasted red peppers from a jar, drained and sliced
- a large handful of fresh coriander, chopped
- salt and ground black pepper

TO SERVE (OPTIONAL)
- guacamole
- sour cream
- grated Cheddar cheese

NUTRITIONAL INFORMATION
Per Serving 379 calories,
7g fat (of which 1g saturates),
40g carbohydrate, 0.6g salt

1 Stack the tortillas, then wrap in foil. Put into the oven, then turn the oven on to 200°C (180°C fan) mark 6 (no need to preheat, as you're just warming the tortillas). Alternatively, wrap the tortillas in clingfilm and microwave on full power for 30 seconds bursts until warmed through.

2 Meanwhile, heat the oil in a large frying pan and fry the garlic and smoked paprika for 30 seconds, then stir in the tomato purée, honey and 4 tbsp water. Add the chicken and sliced peppers and simmer for 5 minutes until piping hot. Stir in most of the chopped coriander and check the seasoning.

3 Spoon the chicken mixture into a dish and garnish with the remaining coriander. Serve the mixture with the warmed tortillas, guacamole, sour cream and grated cheese and let everyone tuck in.

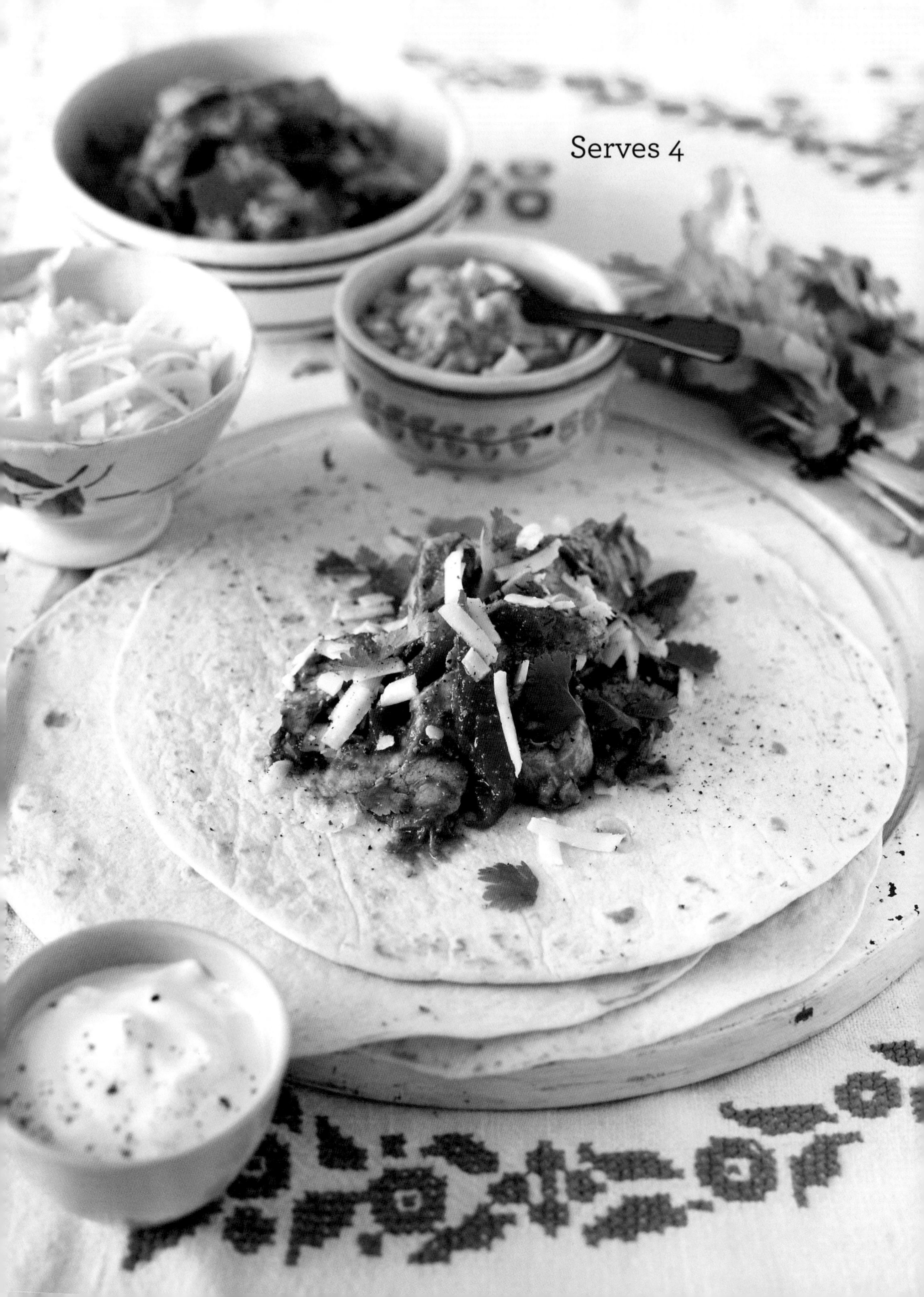
Serves 4

Serves 4

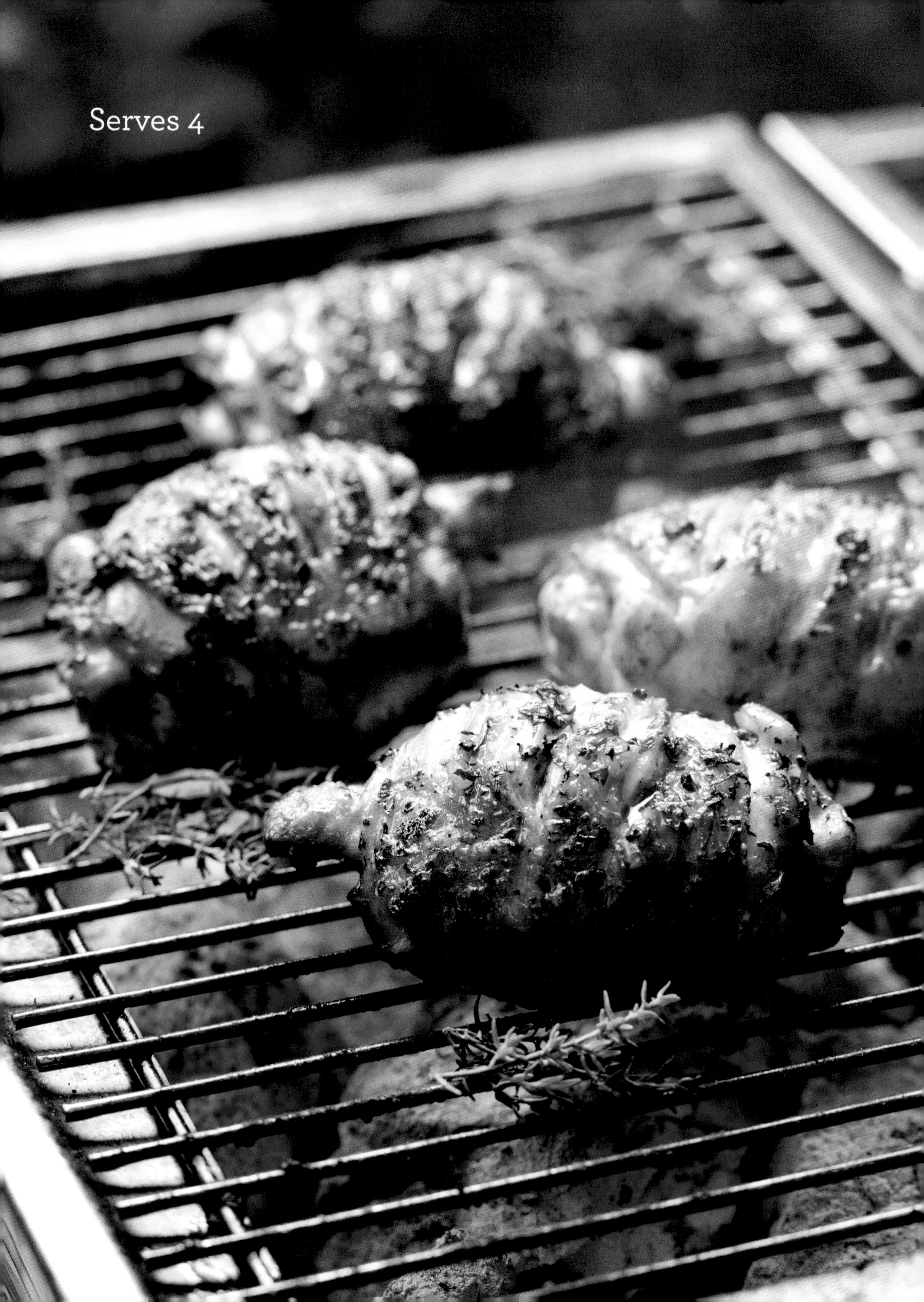

Garlic and Thyme Chicken

Preparation Time
10 minutes
Cooking Time
10–15 minutes

- 2 garlic cloves, crushed
- 2 tbsp freshly chopped thyme leaves, plus extra sprigs to garnish
- 2 tbsp olive oil
- 4 chicken thighs
- salt and ground black pepper

NUTRITIONAL INFORMATION
Per Serving 135 calories,
6g fat (of which 1g saturates),
trace carbohydrate, 0.2g salt

1 Preheat the barbecue or grill. Mix the garlic with the chopped thyme and oil in a large bowl. Season with salt and pepper.

2 Using a sharp knife, make two or three slits in each chicken thigh. Put the chicken into the bowl and toss to coat thoroughly. Barbecue or grill for 5–7 minutes on each side until golden and cooked through. Garnish with thyme sprigs.

Mozzarella, Parma Ham and Rocket Pizza

Preparation Time
10 minutes
Cooking Time
15–18 minutes

- a little plain flour to dust
- 290g pack pizza base mix
- 350g (12oz) fresh tomato and chilli pasta sauce
- 250g (9oz) buffalo mozzarella cheese, drained and roughly chopped
- 6 slices Parma ham, torn into strips
- 50g (2oz) rocket
- a little extra virgin olive oil to drizzle
- salt and ground black pepper

NUTRITIONAL INFORMATION
Per Serving 508 calories, 19.1g fat (of which 10.5g saturates), 64.2g carbohydrate, 1.9g salt

1 Preheat the oven to 200°C (180°C fan oven) mark 6 and lightly flour two large baking sheets. Mix up the pizza base according to the pack instructions. Divide the dough into two and knead each ball on a lightly floured surface for about 5 minutes, then roll them out to make two 23cm (9in) rounds. Put each on to the prepared baking sheet.

2 Divide the tomato sauce between the pizza bases and spread it over, leaving a small border around each edge. Scatter over the mozzarella pieces, then scatter with ham. Season well with salt and pepper.

3 Cook the pizzas for 15–18 minutes until golden. Slide on to a wooden board, top with rocket leaves and drizzle with olive oil. Cut in half to serve.

Cook's Tip
If you're short of time, buy two ready-made pizza bases.

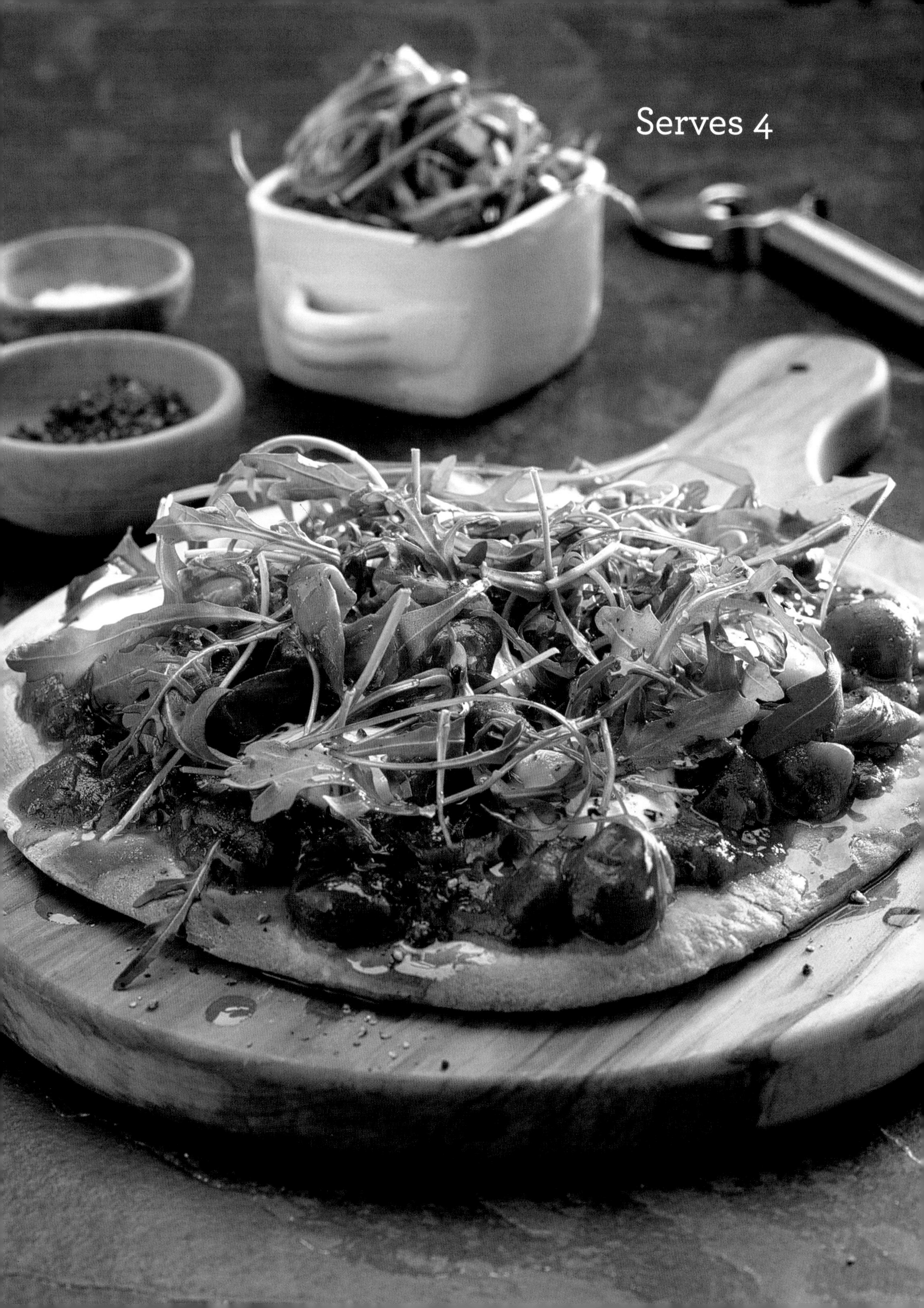
Serves 4

Gammon with Pineapple Salsa

Preparation Time
5 minutes
Cooking Time
about 15 minutes

- 4 × 250g (9oz) gammon steaks
- 1 tbsp sunflower oil
- 250g (9oz) fresh pineapple chunks (or 425g can pineapple chunks in juice, drained)
- 1 red chilli, seeded and finely chopped (see Cook's Tips, page 46)
- a small handful of fresh mint, finely chopped
- salad to serve

NUTRITIONAL INFORMATION
Per Serving **396 calories,**
22g fat (of which 7g saturates),
6g carbohydrate, 0.6g salt

Serves 4

1 Preheat the grill to high. Line two baking sheets with foil. Snip the fat on each gammon steak at 2cm (¾in) intervals and put 2 steaks on each sheet. Brush the oil over the gammon and grill each tray for 6 minutes, turning steaks halfway through the cooking time. Cover the cooked gammon with foil to keep warm.

2 Meanwhile, chop the pineapple chunks into smaller pieces. In a medium bowl, stir the pineapple, chilli and mint together until combined. Serve the gammon, drizzled with any juices, with the pineapple salsa and a salad.

Pork Steaks with Sage and Parma Ham

Preparation Time
5 minutes
Cooking Time
10 minutes

Serves 4

- 4 pork shoulder steaks, about 150g (5oz) each
- 4 thin slices Parma ham or pancetta
- 6 sage leaves
- 1 tbsp oil
- 150ml (¼ pint) pure unsweetened apple juice
- 50g (2oz) chilled butter, diced
- squeeze of lemon juice
- ground black pepper
- steamed cabbage or curly kale and
- mashed sweet potatoes to serve

NUTRITIONAL INFORMATION
Per Serving 328 calories,
20g fat, (of which 9g saturates),
4g carbohydrate, 0.8g salt

Try Something Different
Use white wine instead of apple juice.

1 Put the pork steaks on a board. Lay a slice of Parma ham or pancetta and a sage leaf on each pork steak, then secure to the meat with a wooden cocktail stick. Season with pepper.

2 Heat the oil in a large heavy-based frying pan and fry the pork for about 3–4 minutes on each side until golden brown.

3 Pour in the apple juice, stirring and scraping up the sediment from the base of the pan. Let the liquid bubble until reduced by half. Lift the pork out on to a warmed plate.

4 Return the pan to the heat, add the butter and swirl until melted into the pan juices. Add lemon juice to taste and pour over the pork. Serve with cabbage or curly kale and mashed sweet potatoes.

Serves 4

Herb Sausages with Mustard Dip

Preparation Time
10 minutes
Cooking Time
11 minutes

- 12 sausages
- 12 rashers smoked streaky bacon
- 2 tbsp fresh thyme leaves
- 4 tbsp wholegrain mustard
- 8 tbsp mayonnaise
- 250g (9oz) small tomatoes
- salt and ground black pepper

NUTRITIONAL INFORMATION
Per Serving 836 calories,
76g fat (of which 23g saturates),
16g carbohydrate, 5g salt,

1 Put the sausages in a pan of boiling water, bring back to the boil, reduce the heat and simmer gently for 3 minutes, then drain and leave to cool. Wrap each cold sausage in a rasher of stretched bacon sprinkled with thyme leaves (so the thyme sits next to the sausage) and spear with a wet cocktail stick to secure.

2 Mix together the mustard and mayonnaise and season to taste with salt and pepper.

3 Preheat the barbecue or grill. Cook the sausages for 7–8 minutes until well browned. Barbecue or grill the tomatoes for about 1 minute or until the skins begin to blister and burst.

4 Remove the cocktail sticks from the sausages and serve with the mustard dip and grilled tomatoes.

Try Something Different
You can use any sturdy fresh aromatic herb: oregano or rosemary would make good alternatives to thyme.

Pork Chops with Apple Mash

Preparation Time
5 minutes
Cooking Time
about 15 minutes

- ◆ 4 large potatoes, chopped
- ◆ 4 tsp ready-made spice mix
- ◆ 4 pork chops
- ◆ 25g (1oz) butter
- ◆ a knob of butter
- ◆ 1 red apple, cored and chopped
- ◆ salt and ground black pepper

NUTRITIONAL INFORMATION
Per Serving 532 calories,
26g fat (of which 11g saturates),
37g carbohydrate, 1.6g salt

Serves 4

1 Cook the potatoes in a pan of lightly salted water for 10–12 minutes until tender. Meanwhile, rub the spice mix into the pork chops.

2 Heat the butter in a pan. Add the chops and fry for 5 minutes on each side. Remove from the pan and put on to warm plates. Add a splash of hot water to the pan and swirl the juices around to make a thin gravy. Drain the potatoes.

3 Melt a knob of butter in another pan. Add the chopped apple and fry for 1–2 minutes until starting to soften. Tip the drained potatoes into the pan, season with salt and pepper and mash roughly with the apple. Serve with the chops and gravy.

Herb Lamb Cutlets

Preparation Time
10 minutes
Cooking Time
about 14 minutes

- ◆ 12 lamb cutlets
- ◆ 1½ tbsp Dijon mustard
- ◆ a large handful of fresh parsley, chopped
- ◆ a large handful of fresh mint, chopped
- ◆ salt and ground black pepper
- ◆ boiled new potatoes and a salad to serve

NUTRITIONAL INFORMATION
Per Serving 484 calories,
42g fat (of which 20g saturates),
1g carbohydrate, 0.4g salt

Serves 4

Cook's Tip
Use any combination of chopped fresh herbs you like – coriander, chives and rosemary all work well.

1 Preheat the grill to medium-high. Brush the lamb cutlets with mustard and sprinkle over a little seasoning.

2 Mix the parsley and mint together in a small bowl, then tip on to a plate. Dip each side of the lamb cutlets in the herbs, then put on to a non-stick baking sheet.

3 Grill the lamb for 10–14 minutes (depending on the thickness and how you prefer your meat cooked), turning once. Serve with boiled new potatoes and salad.

Lamb Steaks with Mixed Bean Salad

Preparation Time
5 minutes
Cooking Time
10 minutes

- 150g (5oz) sunblush tomatoes in oil
- 1 garlic clove, crushed
- 2 rosemary sprigs
- 4 × 175g (6oz) leg of lamb steaks
- ½ small red onion, finely sliced
- 2 × 400g cans mixed beans, drained and rinsed
- a large handful of rocket
- salt and ground black pepper

NUTRITIONAL
INFORMATION
Per Serving 545 calories,
20g fat (of which 7g saturates),
30g carbohydrate, 1.8g salt

Serves 4

1   Preheat the grill to high. Drain the sunblush tomatoes, reserving the oil. Put the garlic in a large, shallow dish with 1 tbsp oil from the tomatoes. Strip the leaves from the rosemary sprigs, snip into small pieces and add to the dish. Season with salt and pepper, then add the lamb and toss to coat.

2   Grill the lamb for 3–4 minutes on each side until cooked but still just pink. Meanwhile, roughly chop the tomatoes and put into a pan with the onion, beans, remaining rosemary, rocket and a further 1 tbsp oil from the tomatoes. Warm through until the rocket starts to wilt. Serve the lamb steaks with the bean salad on warmed plates.

Lamb Chops with Crispy Garlic Potatoes

Preparation Time
10 minutes
Cooking Time
20 minutes

Serves 4

- 2 tbsp Mint Sauce (see Cook's Tips)
- 8 small lamb chops
- 3 medium potatoes, cut into 5mm (¼in) slices
- 2 tbsp Garlic-infused Olive Oil (see Cook's Tips)
- 1 tbsp olive oil
- salt and ground black pepper
- steamed green beans to serve

NUTRITIONAL INFORMATION
Per Serving 835 calories,
45g fat (of which 19g saturates),
22g carbohydrate, 0.7g salt

Cook's Tips
Mint Sauce Finely chop 20g
(¾oz) fresh mint and mix with
1 tbsp each olive oil and white
wine vinegar.
Garlic-infused Olive Oil Gently
heat 2 tbsp olive oil with peeled
sliced garlic for 5 minutes and
use immediately. Do not store.

1 Spread the mint sauce over the lamb chops and leave to marinate while you prepare the potatoes.

2 Boil the potatoes in a pan of lightly salted water for 2 minutes or until just starting to soften. Drain, tip back into the pan and season, then add the garlic oil and toss to combine.

3 Meanwhile, heat the olive oil in a large frying pan and fry the chops for 4–5 minutes on each side until just cooked, adding a splash of boiling water to the pan to make a sauce. Remove the chops and sauce from the pan and keep warm.

4 Add the potatoes to the pan. Fry over a medium heat for 10–12 minutes until crisp and golden. Divide the potatoes, chops and sauce among four warmed plates and serve with green beans.

Lamb with Spicy Couscous

Preparation Time
10 minutes
Cooking Time
15 minutes

- ◆ 2 lamb fillets, about 400g (14oz) each
- ◆ 5 tbsp olive oil
- ◆ 1 aubergine, cut into 1cm (½in) dice
- ◆ 1 tsp ground cumin
- ◆ ½ tsp ground cinnamon
- ◆ 225g (8oz) quick-cook couscous
- ◆ 1 large fresh red chilli, seeded and finely chopped (see Cook's Tips, page 46)
- ◆ 3 tbsp freshly chopped mint
- ◆ 75g (3oz) raisins, soaked in hot water and drained
- ◆ salt and ground black pepper
- ◆ Greek yogurt to serve

NUTRITIONAL INFORMATION
Per Serving 675 calories,
37g fat (of which 13g saturates),
44g carbohydrate, 0.5g salt

1 Trim the lamb fillets, rub in 1 tbsp oil and season well with salt and pepper. Heat a heavy-based non-stick pan, add the lamb and fry for 15 minutes, turning regularly. Remove from the pan and leave to rest for 5 minutes (see Cook's Tip).

2 Meanwhile, toss the aubergine in the cumin and cinnamon, then fry in 2 tbsp oil for 10 minutes or until softened. Prepare the couscous according to the pack instructions, then fluff the grains using a fork. Add the aubergine, chilli, 2 tbsp mint, the raisins and the remaining oil to the couscous. Season well with salt and pepper.

3 To serve, slice the lamb and place on top of the couscous. Drizzle with Greek yogurt, sprinkle with the remaining chopped mint and serve immediately.

Cook's Tip
Leaving the lamb to rest for 5 minutes allows the juices to set and they won't run out.

Serves 4

Crisp Crumbed Lamb Cutlets

Preparation Time
20 minutes
Cooking Time
10 minutes

- 75g (3oz) breadcrumbs, made from one-day-old bread
- 40g (1½oz) Parma ham, finely chopped
- 3 tbsp freshly grated Parmesan
- 8 lamb cutlets, well trimmed, or 2 French-trimmed racks of lamb, about 350g (12oz) each, divided into cutlets
- 2 eggs, beaten
- 3 tbsp oil
- 3 large garlic cloves, peeled but left whole
- salt and ground black pepper
- tomato relish, new potatoes and a salad or green vegetable to serve

NUTRITIONAL INFORMATION
Per Serving 639 calories,
51g fat (of which 21g saturates),
15g carbohydrate, 1.9g salt

Serves 4

1 Mix together the breadcrumbs, Parma ham and Parmesan, spread out on a large plate and put to one side.

2 Season the lamb with salt and pepper, and brush lightly with beaten egg. Press the lamb into the breadcrumbs to coat evenly, but lightly.

3 Heat the oil in a large non-stick frying pan, add the peeled garlic cloves and heat gently until golden brown, then discard the garlic.

4 Fry the lamb in the garlic-infused oil over a low-medium heat for 4–5 minutes on each side until deep golden brown and crisp. Turn and fry the fat edge for 1–2 minutes.

5 Serve the cutlets with tomato relish, new potatoes and a salad or green vegetable.

Quick Beef Stroganoff

Preparation Time
10 minutes
Cooking Time
20 minutes

Serves 4

- ◆ 700g (1½lb) rump or fillet steak, trimmed
- ◆ 50g (2oz) unsalted butter or 4 tbsp olive oil
- ◆ 1 onion, thinly sliced
- ◆ 225g (8oz) brown-cap mushrooms, sliced
- ◆ 3 tbsp brandy
- ◆ 1 tsp French mustard
- ◆ 200ml (7fl oz) crème fraîche
- ◆ 100ml (3½fl oz) double cream
- ◆ 3 tbsp freshly chopped flat-leafed parsley
- ◆ salt and ground black pepper
- ◆ rice or noodles to serve

NUTRITIONAL INFORMATION
Per Serving 750 calories, 60g fat (of which 35g saturates), 3g carbohydrate, 0.5g salt

Freezing Tip
Complete the recipe, transfer to a freezerproof container, cool, label and freeze for up to three months. Thaw overnight in the fridge. Put into a pan, cover and bring to the boil, then reduce the heat and simmer until piping hot.

1 Cut the steak into strips about 5mm (¼in) wide and 5cm (2in) long.

2 Heat half the butter or oil in a large heavy frying pan over a medium heat. Add the onion and cook gently for 10 minutes or until soft and golden. Remove with a slotted spoon and put to one side. Add the mushrooms to the pan and cook, stirring, for 2–3 minutes until golden brown. Remove and put to one side.

3 Increase the heat and and add the remaining butter or oil to the pan. Quickly fry the meat, in two or three batches, for 2–3 minutes, stirring constantly to ensure even browning. Add the brandy and allow it to bubble to reduce.

4 Put the meat, onion and mushrooms back into the pan. Reduce the heat and stir in the mustard, crème fraîche and cream. Heat through, stir in most of the parsley and season with salt and pepper. Serve with rice or noodles, with the remaining parsley scattered over the top.

Serves 4

Sesame Beef

Preparation Time
10 minutes
Cooking Time
10 minutes

- 2 tbsp soy sauce
- 2 tbsp Worcestershire sauce
- 2 tsp tomato purée
- juice of ½ lemon
- 1 tbsp sesame seeds
- 1 garlic clove, crushed
- 400g (14oz) rump steak, sliced
- 1 tbsp vegetable oil
- 3 small pak choi, chopped
- 1 bunch spring onions, sliced
- freshly cooked egg noodles or tagliatelle to serve

NUTRITIONAL INFORMATION
Per Serving 207 calories,
10g fat (of which 3g saturates),
4g carbohydrate, 2g salt,

1 Mix the soy sauce, Worcestershire sauce, tomato purée, lemon juice, sesame seeds and garlic together in a bowl. Add the steak and toss to coat.

2 Heat the oil in a large wok or non-stick frying pan until hot. Add the steak and sear well. Remove from the wok and put to one side.

3 Add any sauce from the bowl to the wok and heat for 1 minute. Add the pak choi, spring onions and steak, and stir-fry for 5 minutes. Add freshly cooked and drained noodles or pasta, toss and serve immediately.

Try Something Different
Use 400g (14oz) pork escalope cut into strips instead of beef. Cook for 5 minutes before removing from the pan at step 2.

Sesame Beef Skewers with Noodle Salad

Preparation Time
10 minutes
Cooking Time
about 5 minutes

- 3 × 300g (11oz) rump steak, fat trimmed
- 2 tbsp oyster sauce
- 1 tsp Chinese five-spice powder
- ½ tbsp sesame seeds
- 300g bag straight-to-wok rice vermicelli
- ½ cucumber, finely diced
- 1 chilli, seeded and finely chopped (see Cook's Tips, page 46)
- 2 tbsp toasted sesame oil
- grated zest and juice of 1 lime
- 2 tbsp soy sauce
- a large handful of fresh coriander, roughly chopped, plus extra sprigs to garnish
- salt and ground black pepper
- lime wedges to serve
- 12 metal or presoaked wooden skewers

NUTRITIONAL INFORMATION
Per Serving 563 calories,
16g fat (of which 5g saturates),
49g carbohydrate, 1.1g salt

1 Preheat the grill to high. Cut the beef into 2.5cm (1in) thick strips and put into a bowl. Stir through the oyster sauce, five-spice powder and some seasoning. Thread the strips on to the wooden skewers, then arrange on a baking sheet and sprinkle over the sesame seeds. Grill for 4–5 minutes, turning once, for medium (cook for a shorter or longer time depending on your preference).

2 Meanwhile, put the noodles into a colander and pour over a kettle of boiling water. Rinse quickly under cold water and drain. Put into a bowl and toss through the cucumber, chilli, toasted sesame oil, lime zest and juice, soy sauce and coriander. Garnish the beef with coriander and serve with lime wedges and the noodle salad.

Fillet Steak with Madeira Sauce

Preparation Time
10 minutes
Cooking Time
about 15 minutes

- 1 tbsp sunflower oil
- 4 fillet steaks, about 150g (5oz) each
- 150ml (5fl oz) Madeira
- 200ml (7fl oz) hot beef stock
- 100ml (3½fl oz) double cream
- 1 tsp Dijon mustard
- salt and ground black pepper
- seasonal vegetables to serve

NUTRITIONAL INFORMATION
Per Serving 413 calories,
26g fat (of which 13g saturates),
3g carbohydrate, 0.5g salt

Serves 4

COOK'S TIP
This versatile sauce is also excellent served with pan-fried lamb, pork, pheasant or chicken breasts – simply replace the beef stock with lamb or chicken stock.

1 Heat the oil in a pan over a medium-high heat and fry the steaks for 2¼ minutes on each side for rare and 3¼ minutes on each side for medium rare. Put to one side on a warm plate and cover loosely with foil. Leave to rest for at least 10 minutes while you make the sauce.

2 Pour the Madeira into the same pan and simmer rapidly until syrupy, scraping the crusty bits from the base of the pan – these contain lots of flavour. Add the stock and simmer for 4–5 minutes, then add any juices from the resting steaks.

3 Add the cream and bubble for 1–2 minutes until thickened. Stir in the mustard and check the seasoning. Serve the steaks with seasonal vegetables and a little of the sauce drizzled over.

Steak with Blue Cheese and Mushroom Pappardelle

Preparation Time
15 minutes
Cooking Time
about 15 minutes

Serves 4

- ◆ 350g (12oz) dried pappardelle pasta
- ◆ 1tbsp sunflower oil
- ◆ 2 × 300g (11oz) rump steaks
- ◆ 250g (9oz) chestnut mushrooms, sliced
- ◆ 200g (7oz) half-fat crème fraîche
- ◆ 40g (1½oz) blue cheese, plus extra to garnish
- ◆ 100g (3½oz) baby leaf spinach
- ◆ 25g (1oz) walnuts, chopped, to garnish
- ◆ salt and ground black pepper

NUTRITIONAL INFORMATION
Per Serving 655 calories,
23g fat (of which 9g saturates),
69g carbohydrate, 0.5g salt

1 Bring a large pan of salted water to the boil and cook the pasta according to the pack instructions. Heat half the oil in a large frying pan over a high heat. Pat the steaks dry with kitchen paper, season well and fry for 5–6 minutes for medium meat, turning once (cook for shorter/longer if you prefer). Lift the steaks out of the pan and put to one side on a board.

2 Carefully wipe the empty pan clean with kitchen paper. Return to the heat and add the remaining oil. Fry the mushrooms for 5 minutes until softened. Stir in the crème fraîche and blue cheese and leave to melt. Meanwhile, slice the steaks.

3 Drain the cooked pasta, reserving a cupful of the cooking water. Return the pasta to the empty pan, then toss through the sauce, sliced steak and spinach. If needed, add some of the pasta cooking water to slacken the mixture. Check the seasoning, then divide among four plates and garnish with walnuts and a little extra crumbled blue cheese. Serve immediately.

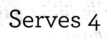
Serves 4

Steak au Poivre

Preparation Time
10 minutes
Cooking Time
4–12 minutes

- 2 tbsp black or green peppercorns
- 4 rump or sirloin steaks, 200g (7oz) each
- 25g (1oz) butter
- 1 tbsp oil
- 2 tbsp brandy
- 150ml (¼ pint) double cream or crème fraîche
- salt
- herbed roast potatoes and green beans to serve

NUTRITIONAL INFORMATION
Per Serving 480 calories,
35g fat (of which 19g saturates),
1g carbohydrate, 1g salt

1 Crush the peppercorns coarsely using a pestle and mortar or a rolling pin. Scatter the peppercorns on a board, lay the steaks on top and press hard to encrust the surface of the meat; repeat with the other side.

2 Heat the butter and oil in a frying pan and quickly sear the steaks over a high heat. Reduce the heat to medium and cook for a further 3–12 minutes, according to taste, turning every 2 minutes (see Cook's Tip). Season with salt.

3 Remove the steaks from the pan; keep warm. Add the brandy to the pan, remove from the heat and set alight. When the flame dies, stir in the cream or crème fraîche, season and reheat gently. Pour the sauce over the steaks and serve with roast potatoes and green beans.

Try Something Different
Steak Diane Trim 4 pieces of fillet steak, 5mm (¼in) thick, of excess fat. Fry the steaks in 25g (1oz) butter and 2 tbsp vegetable oil for 1–2 minutes on each side. Remove with a slotted spoon and keep warm. Stir 2 tbsp Worcestershire sauce and 1 tbsp lemon juice into the pan juices. Warm through, then add 1 small onion, peeled and grated and 2 tsp freshly chopped parsley, and cook gently for 1 minute. Serve the sauce spooned over the steaks.

Cook's Tip
Allow 4 minutes (one turn) for rare steaks; 8 minutes (three turns) for medium. For well-done, 12 minutes, increasing the time between turns to 3 minutes.

Pheasant Curry

Preparation Time
15 minutes, plus optional
marinating
Cooking Time
about 10 minutes

- 2 tsp coriander seeds
- 1 tsp each cumin seeds,
  ground turmeric and ground
  cinnamon
- ¼ tsp dried chilli flakes
- a good pinch of saffron
  threads
- 2 garlic cloves, roughly
  chopped
- 2.5cm (1in) piece fresh root
  ginger, peeled and grated
- 6 skinless pheasant breasts,
  cut into bite-sized pieces
- ½ tbsp olive oil
- 165ml can full-fat coconut
  milk
- salt and ground black pepper
- a large handful of fresh
  coriander, roughly chopped,
  to garnish
- naan or cooked rice to serve

**NUTRITIONAL
INFORMATION**
Per Serving 423 calories,
16g fat (of which 9g saturates),
1g carbohydrate, 0.3g salt

1 Put the coriander seeds, cumin seeds, turmeric, ground cinnamon, chilli flakes, saffron, garlic, ginger and some salt into a pestle and mortar and bash together until you have a well-combined pulp. Rub the spice mixture into the pheasant pieces and leave to marinate for 10 minutes, if you have time.

2 Heat the oil in a large pan and add the marinated pheasant. Brown for a few minutes, then add the coconut milk and 150ml (¼ pint) water. Bring to the boil, then reduce the heat and simmer for 5 minutes.

3 Check the seasoning, garnish with coriander and serve with naan or rice.

Serves 4

Puddings and Sweet Treats

Nectarines in Spiced Honey and Lemon

Preparation Time
10 minutes, plus cooling

- ◆ 4 tbsp clear honey
- ◆ 2 star anise
- ◆ 1 tbsp freshly squeezed lemon juice
- ◆ 150ml (¼ pint) boiling water
- ◆ 4 ripe nectarines or peaches, halved and stoned
- ◆ vanilla ice cream to serve

NUTRITIONAL INFORMATION
Per Serving 95 calories, trace fat (of which 0g saturates), 23g carbohydrate, 0g salt

Serves 4

Try Something Different
Use a cinnamon stick instead of the star anise.

1 Put the honey, star anise and lemon juice in a heatproof bowl. Stir in the boiling water and leave until just warm.

2 Add the nectarines or peaches to the bowl and leave to cool. Transfer to a glass serving dish. Serve with a scoop of vanilla ice cream.

White Chocolate and Berry Crêpes

Preparation Time
2 minutes
Cooking Time
10 minutes

- 500g bag frozen mixed berries, thawed
- 100g (3½oz) good-quality white chocolate, broken into pieces
- 142ml carton double cream
- 4 thin ready-made crêpes

NUTRITIONAL INFORMATION
Per Serving 476 calories, 37g fat (of which 15g saturates), 37g carbohydrate, 0.2g salt

Cook's Tip
Instead of mixed berries, try using just one type of berry.

Serves 4

1 Put the thawed berries into a large pan and cook over a medium heat for 5 minutes or until heated through.

2 Meanwhile, put the chocolate and cream into a heatproof bowl set over a pan of simmering water, making sure the bottom of the bowl doesn't touch the hot water. Heat gently, stirring, for 5 minutes or until the chocolate has just melted. Remove the bowl from the pan and mix the chocolate and cream to a smooth sauce. Alternatively, microwave the chocolate and the cream together on full power for 2–2½ minutes (based on a 900W oven), then stir until smooth.

3 Meanwhile, heat the crêpes according to the pack instructions.

4 To serve, put each crêpe on a warmed plate and fold in half. Spoon a quarter of the berries into the middle of each, then fold the crêpe over the filling and pour the hot chocolate sauce over the top.

Serves 4

Amaretti with Lemon Mascarpone

Preparation Time
15 minutes
Cooking Time
5 minutes

- finely sliced zest and juice of ¼ lemon (see Cook's Tips)
- 1 tbsp golden caster sugar, plus a little extra to sprinkle
- 50g (2oz) mascarpone cheese
- 12 amaretti biscuits

NUTRITIONAL INFORMATION
Per Serving 180 calories,
8g fat (of which 4g saturates),
28g carbohydrate, 0.4g salt,

1 Put the lemon juice into a small pan. Add the sugar and dissolve over a low heat. Once the sugar has dissolved, add the lemon zest and cook for 1–2 minutes – it will curl up. Using a slotted spoon, lift out the zest strips and lay them on a sheet of baking parchment, reserving the syrup. Sprinkle the strips with sugar to coat.

2 Beat the mascarpone in a bowl to soften, then stir in the reserved sugar syrup.

3 Put a blob of mascarpone on each amaretti biscuit, then top with a couple of strips of the crystallised lemon peel.

Cook's Tips
To prepare the strips of zest, pare the rind from the lemon, remove any white pith, and finely slice the zest into long strips.
If you're short of time, buy a pack of crystallised lemon slices and use these to decorate the pudding. Alternatively, decorate each biscuit with a little finely grated lemon zest.

Baked Apricots with Almonds

Preparation Time
5 minutes
Cooking Time
20–25 minutes

- 12 apricots, halved and stoned
- 3 tbsp golden caster sugar
- 2 tbsp amaretto liqueur
- 25g (1oz) unsalted butter
- 25g (1oz) flaked almonds
- crème fraîche to serve

**NUTRITIONAL
INFORMATION**
Per Serving 124 calories,
6g fat (of which 2g saturates),
16g carbohydrate, 0.1g salt,

1 Preheat the oven to 200°C (180°C fan oven) mark 6. Put the apricot halves, cut side up, in an ovenproof dish. Sprinkle with the sugar, drizzle with the liqueur, then dot each apricot half with a little butter. Scatter the flaked almonds over them.

2 Bake in the oven for 20–25 minutes until the apricots are soft and the juices are syrupy. Serve warm, with crème fraîche.

Try Something Different
Use nectarines or peaches instead of apricots.

Serves 6

Serves 4

Quick Gooey Chocolate Puddings

Preparation Time
15 minutes
Cooking Time
12–15 minutes

- ◆ 100g (3½oz) unsalted butter, plus extra to grease
- ◆ 100g (3½oz) golden caster sugar, plus extra to dust
- ◆ 100g (3½oz) plain chocolate (at least 70% cocoa solids), broken into pieces
- ◆ 2 large eggs
- ◆ 20g (¾oz) plain flour
- ◆ icing sugar to dust
- ◆ whipped cream to serve

NUTRITIONAL INFORMATION
Per Serving 468 calories,
31g fat (of which 19g saturates),
46g carbohydrate, 0.6g salt

1 Preheat the oven to 200°C (180°C fan oven) mark 6. Butter four 200ml (7fl oz) ramekins and dust with sugar. Melt the chocolate and butter in a heatproof bowl set over a pan of gently simmering water, making sure the base of the bowl doesn't touch the water. Take the bowl off the pan and leave to cool for 5 minutes.

2 Whisk the eggs, caster sugar and flour together in a bowl until smooth. Fold in the chocolate mixture and pour into the ramekins.

3 Stand the dishes on a baking tray and bake for 12–15 minutes until the puddings are puffed and set on the outside, but still runny inside.

4 Turn the puddings out, dust with icing sugar and serve immediately with whipped cream.

Mango Gratin with Sabayon

Preparation Time
5 minutes, plus optional
10 minutes resting
Cooking Time
10 minutes

- 3 large ripe mangoes, peeled, stoned and sliced
- 5 medium egg yolks
- 6 tbsp golden caster sugar
- 300ml (½ pint) champagne or sparkling wine
- 6 tbsp dark muscovado sugar to sprinkle
- crisp sweet biscuits to serve

NUTRITIONAL INFORMATION
Per Serving 249 calories,
5g fat (of which 1g saturates),
45g carbohydrate, 0g salt

Serves 6

1 Arrange the mangoes in six serving glasses. Whisk the egg yolks and caster sugar in a large heatproof bowl over a pan of gently simmering water until the mixture is thick and falls in soft ribbon shapes. Add the champagne or sparkling wine and continue to whisk until the mixture is thick and foamy again. Remove from the heat.

2 Spoon the sabayon over the mangoes, sprinkle with the muscovado sugar, then leave for 10 minutes to go fudgey. Serve with biscuits.

Cinnamon Pancakes

Preparation Time
5 minutes, plus standing
Cooking Time
20 minutes

- 150g (5oz) plain flour
- ½ tsp ground cinnamon
- 1 medium egg
- 300ml (½ pint) skimmed milk
- olive oil to fry
- fruit compote or sugar and Greek yogurt to serve

NUTRITIONAL INFORMATION
Per Serving 141 calories,
5g fat (of which 1g saturates),
20g carbohydrate, 0.1g salt

Serves 6

1 Whisk the flour, cinnamon, egg and milk together in a large bowl to make a smooth batter. Leave to stand for 20 minutes.

2 Heat a heavy-based frying pan over a medium heat. When the pan is really hot, add 1 tsp oil, pour in a ladleful of batter and tilt the pan to coat the base with an even layer. Cook for 1 minute or until golden. Flip over and cook for 1 minute. Repeat with the remaining batter, adding more oil if necessary, to make six pancakes. Serve with a fruit compote or a sprinkling of sugar, and a dollop of yogurt.

Chocolate Torte

Preparation Time
15 minutes, plus cooling

- ◆ 200g (7oz) plain chocolate, broken into pieces
- ◆ 25g (1oz) butter, melted, plus extra to grease
- ◆ 1½ tbsp golden syrup
- ◆ 125g (4oz) butter biscuits, finely crushed
- ◆ 40g (1½oz) icing sugar
- ◆ 300ml (½ pint) double cream, at room temperature
- ◆ 2–3 tbsp Amaretto (optional)
- ◆ crème fraîche to serve

TO DECORATE
- ◆ plain chocolate, grated
- ◆ raspberries
- ◆ icing sugar to dust

NUTRITIONAL INFORMATION
Per Serving 383 calories,
27 fat (of which 16g saturates),
31g carbohydrate, 0.3g salt

1 Melt the chocolate in a heatproof bowl set over a pan of barely simmering water. Leave to cool for 10 minutes. Grease and line the sides of a 20.5cm (8in) loose-bottomed cake tin with greaseproof paper.

2 Mix the butter, golden syrup and crushed biscuits together in a medium bowl. Press the mixture into the base of the prepared tin.

3 Sift the icing sugar into a separate bowl. Pour in the cream and Amaretto (if using) and whip until the cream just holds its shape. Using a metal spoon, fold the cooled chocolate into the cream mix. Spoon the chocolate mix into the cake tin, level the surface, cover and chill until ready to serve.

4 Transfer the torte to a serving plate. Peel off the paper and scatter grated chocolate over the top. Dot over a few raspberries and lightly dust with icing sugar. Serve in slices with crème fraîche.

Get Ahead
Complete the recipe to the end of step 3 up to one day in advance. Complete the ecipe to serve.

Serves 10

Serves 6

Cheat's Tiramisu

Preparation Time
15 minutes

- 375g (13oz) mascarpone
- 75g (3oz) plain chocolate, finely chopped
- 2 medium eggs
- 75g (3oz) caster sugar
- 175g–200g (6–7oz) chocolate loaf cake or brownies, roughly chopped
- 6 tbsp Tia Maria liqueur
- cocoa powder to dust
- gold leaf to sprinkle

NUTRITIONAL INFORMATION
Per Serving 614 calories, 43g fat (of which 23g saturates), 45g carbohydrate, 0.9g salt

1 Mix the mascarpone and chocolate together in a large bowl until combined. In a separate medium bowl, beat together the eggs and sugar using hand-held electric beaters for about 5 minutes until pale and moussey. Use a large metal spoon to fold egg mixture into the mascarpone bowl.

2 Divide half the chocolate loaf cake or brownies among six large glasses, then drizzle ½ tbsp Tia Maria into each glass. Next, divide half the mascarpone mixture equally among the glasses. Repeat the layering process once more.

3 Cut a star template from a sheet of paper. Lay over one glass and dust with cocoa powder. Repeat with remaining glasses and sprinkle gold leaf over each pudding. Serve immediately.

Note
As this pudding contains raw eggs, buy those that carry the British Lion Mark and don't serve to vulnerable groups.

Luscious Chocolate Pots

Preparation Time
5 minutes
Cooking Time
about 3 minutes

- 175g (6oz) condensed milk
- 75g (3oz) plain chocolate, finely chopped
- 1–2 tsp almond liqueur, plus extra for drizzling (optional)
- 150ml (¼ pint) double cream
- plain chocolate shavings and almond biscuits to serve

NUTRITIONAL INFORMATION
Per Serving 484 calories,
31g fat (of which 19g saturates),
42g carbohydrate, 0.2g salt

1 Put the condensed milk into a small pan and warm over a low heat until just bubbling at the edges. Take off the heat and stir in the chocolate. Add the liqueur (if using) and mix until smooth and shiny. Put into a large bowl and stir for 1 minute or until cool.

2 In a separate bowl, whip the cream until it just holds its shape – don't overwhip or it will turn grainy. Using a large metal spoon, gently fold the cream into the chocolate mixture until well combined.

3 Divide the mixture among four small glasses and sprinkle chocolate shavings and a little liqueur over each (if using). Serve immediately with almond biscuits.

Serves 4

Serves 8

Raspberry Meringue Pie

Preparation Time
15 minutes
Cooking Time
about 8 minutes

- 8 trifle sponges
- 450g (1lb) frozen raspberries, thawed and lightly crushed
- 2–3 tbsp raspberry liqueur
- 3 medium egg whites
- 150g (5oz) golden caster sugar

NUTRITIONAL INFORMATION
Per Serving 252 calories,
3g fat (of which trace saturates),
49g carbohydrate, 0.1g salt

1 Preheat the oven to 230°C (210°C fan) mark 8. Put the sponges in the bottom of a 2 litre (3½ pint) ovenproof dish. Spread the raspberries on top and drizzle over the raspberry liqueur.

2 Whisk the egg whites in a clean bowl until stiff peaks form. Gradually whisk in the sugar until the mixture is smooth and glossy. Spoon the meringue mixture over the raspberries in the dish and bake for 6–8 minutes until golden.

Luscious Lemon Passion Pots

Preparation Time
5 minutes

- 150g (5oz) condensed milk
- 50ml (2fl oz) double cream
- grated zest and juice of 1 large lemon
- 1 passion fruit

NUTRITIONAL INFORMATION
Per Serving **377 calories,**
21g fat (of which 13g saturates),
43g carbohydrate, 0.3g salt

1 Put the condensed milk, double cream and lemon zest and juice into a medium bowl and whisk until thick and fluffy. Spoon into two small ramekins or coffee cups and chill until needed – or carry on with the recipe if you can't wait.

2 To serve, halve the passion fruit, scoop out the seeds and use to decorate the lemon pots.

Serves 2

Serves 4

Boozy Eton Mess

Preparation Time
10 minutes
Cooking Time
about 5 minutes, plus cooling

- ½ tsp arrowroot
- 125ml (4fl oz) crème de cassis
- 300ml (½ pint) double cream
- 2–3 tbsp icing sugar, sifted
- ½ tsp vanilla extract
- 25g (1oz) meringue nests, broken up
- 150g (5oz) blueberries
- 15g (½oz) flaked almonds

NUTRITIONAL INFORMATION
Per Serving 553 calories,
43g fat (of which 25g saturates),
31g carbohydrate, 0g salt

1 Put the arrowroot into a small pan and gradually whisk in the crème de cassis. Put the pan over a high heat and simmer for 1–2 minutes, whisking constantly, until the syrup thickens. Take off the heat, empty into a small jug, and leave to cool.

2 Pour the cream into a large bowl. Add the icing sugar and vanilla, and whip until the cream just holds its shape – don't overwhip or it will turn grainy.

3 Divide the meringues among four large glasses. Spoon a few blueberries into each glass, then drizzle a little of the cassis syrup over them. Next, divide the cream equally among the glasses and top each with a quarter each of the remaining blueberries and cassis syrup. Sprinkle over the almonds and serve immediately.

Quick Christmas Pudding

Preparation Time
15 minutes
Cooking Time
about 10 minutes

- 100g (3½oz) butter, softened, plus extra to grease
- 100g (3½oz) ready-made cranberry sauce
- 2 tbsp golden syrup
- 100g (3½oz) dark brown soft sugar
- 2 medium eggs, beaten
- 100g (3½oz) plain flour
- 1 heaped tbsp mixed spice
- 300g (11oz) mixed dried fruit
- 1 medium apple, peeled and grated

NUTRITIONAL INFORMATION
Per Serving 451 calories,
17g fat (of which 9g saturates),
76g carbohydrate, 0.4g salt

1 Grease a 1.2 litre (2¼ pint) pudding basin. In a small bowl, stir together the cranberry sauce and golden syrup. Spoon two-thirds of the mixture into the base of the prepared basin, reserving the remaining mixture.

2 In a separate bowl, beat together the butter, sugar, eggs, flour, mixed spice, dried fruit and grated apple until well combined. Spoon the mixture into the prepared basin and press a large piece of parchment paper on to the pudding to cover the surface.

3 Microwave on medium power for 9 minutes until firm to the touch. Leave to stand for 10 minutes before turning out on to a plate. Spoon over the reserved cranberry mixture and serve immediately.

Get Ahead
Complete the recipe to the end of step 2 up to 2 hours in advance. Leave at room temperature. Complete the recipe to serve.

Don't have a microwave?
Complete the recipe to the end of step 2 but don't cover with parchment paper. Instead, put a large square of foil over one of the same size of greaseproof paper. Fold a pleat in the middle of both, then cover the basin, foil side up, and secure with string. Put an upturned heatproof saucer in a deep pan, then balance the pudding on top. Fill the pan with water so it comes halfway up the sides of the basin. Bring to the boil then reduce the heat to a gentle simmer. Cover with a tight-fitting lid and cook for 1½ hours, topping up the water as necessary.

Serves 6

Serves 6

Cheat's Chocolate Soufflés

Preparation Time
15 minutes
Cooking Time
about 10–12 minutes

- ◆ butter to grease
- ◆ 75g (3oz) plain chocolate
- ◆ 225ml (8fl oz) fresh chocolate custard
- ◆ 3 medium egg whites
- ◆ 25g (1oz) caster sugar
- ◆ icing sugar, to dust

NUTRITIONAL INFORMATION
Per Serving **126 calories,**
5g fat (of which 2g saturates),
19g carbohydrate, 0.1g salt

1 Preheat the oven to 220°C (200°C fan) mark 7. Put a baking sheet on the middle shelf to heat up, making sure there's enough space for the soufflés to rise. Grease six 125ml (4fl oz) ramekins.

2 Finely grate the chocolate, or whiz until it resembles breadcrumbs. Dust the insides of the ramekins with 25g (1oz) of the chocolate.

3 Mix the custard and remaining chocolate together in a large bowl. In a separate bowl, whisk the egg whites until stiff but not dry, then gradually add the caster sugar to the egg whites, whisking well after each addition. Using a metal spoon, fold the egg whites into the custard mixture.

4 Quickly divide the mixture among the prepared ramekins, put them on to the preheated baking sheet and bake for 10–12 minutes until well risen. Dust the soufflés with icing sugar and serve immediately.

Tutti Frutti Sorbet

Preparation Time
10 minutes

- 450g (1lb) frozen fruit of your choice, such as blueberries, raspberries, summer fruits or mango
- 75g (3oz) icing sugar
- 1 tbsp fruit liqueur, such as framboise or cassis, plus extra to drizzle (optional)
- Chopped nuts, grated chocolate or chopped fresh mint to decorate (optional)

NUTRITIONAL INFORMATION
Per Serving, using liqueur
110 calories, 0.1g fat (of which 0g saturates), 27g carbohydrate, 0g salt

1 Put the frozen fruit and icing sugar into a food processor or blender, pour in the liqueur (if using) or add 1 tbsp water and whiz for 1–2 minutes until smooth and scoopable. Be patient – it may take a while for the fruit to break up.

2 Spoon the sorbet into bowls or glasses and drizzle with extra liqueur, or decorate with chopped nuts, grated chocolate or mint, if you like. Serve immediately or freeze in an airtight container for up to three months.

Serves 4

Sticky Banoffee Pies

Preparation Time
15 minutes

- 150g (5oz) digestive biscuits
- 75g (3oz) unsalted butter, melted, plus butter to grease
- 1 tsp ground ginger (optional)
- 450g (1lb) dulce de leche toffee sauce
- 4 medium-sized bananas, peeled, sliced and tossed in the juice of 1 lemon
- 285ml (9½fl oz) double cream, softly whipped
- plain chocolate shavings

NUTRITIONAL INFORMATION
Per Serving 827 calories,
55g fat (of which 32g saturates),
84g carbs, 1.2g salt

Serves 6

Finishing touches
Finish the banoffee pies with any kind of chocolate decorations you like. Grated chocolate, chocolate shavings and curls all look good.

1 Put the biscuits in a food processor and whiz to a crumb. (Alternatively, put them in a plastic bag and crush with a rolling pin. Transfer to a bowl.) Add the melted butter and ginger and process, or stir well, for 1 minute to combine.

2 Grease six 10cm (4in) rings or tartlet tins and line with greaseproof paper. Press the biscuit mixture into each ring. Divide the toffee sauce equally among the rings and top with the bananas. Pipe or spoon on the cream, sprinkle with chocolate shavings and chill. Remove from the rings or tins to serve.

Chocolate-dipped Strawberries

Preparation Time
10 minutes

- 100g (3½oz) milk chocolate, broken into chunks
- 100g (3½oz) white chocolate, broken into chunks
- 100g (3½oz) plain chocolate (at least 70% cocoa solids), broken into chunks
- 700g (1½lb) strawberries

NUTRITIONAL INFORMATION
Per Serving 291 calories, 15g fat (of which 9g saturates), 37g carbs, 0.1g salt

1 Put each type of chocolate side by side in a single heatproof bowl, keeping each type as separate as you can.

2 Melt the chocolate over a pan of gently simmering water, then dip each strawberry into the chocolate, holding it by its stalk. Arrange the strawberries in a shallow bowl to serve. Alternatively let everyone dunk the berries themselves.

Warm Caramel Puddings

Preparation Time
10 minutes
Cooking Time
about 15 minutes, plus cooling

- 100g (3½oz) unsalted butter, chopped, plus extra for greasing
- 125g (4oz) good-quality plain chocolate (70% cocoa solids), chopped
- 2 medium eggs
- 2 medium egg yolks
- 40g (1½oz) caster sugar
- 40g (1½oz) plain flour
- 4–8 squares of caramel-centre chocolate
- crème fraîche, to serve

NUTRITIONAL INFORMATION
Per Serving 670 calories,
51g fat (of which 29g saturates),
45g carbohydrate, 0.1g salt

1 Preheat the oven to 200°C (180°C fan) mark 6. Grease four 200ml (7fl oz) ramekins.

2 Melt the plain chocolate and butter together in a heatproof bowl set over a pan of barely simmering water, making sure the bowl does not touch the water. Leave to cool for 5 minutes.

3 Meanwhile, put the whole eggs, egg yolks and caster sugar into a large bowl and whisk with a hand-held electric whisk for 5–6 minutes until moussey and thick. Sift the flour over the mixture, then fold it in using a large metal spoon. Next, fold in the cooled chocolate mixture. Spoon into the prepared ramekins and gently push 1–2 pieces of caramel chocolate into the top of each pudding.

4 Put the ramekins on to a baking sheet and bake the puddings for 8–10 minutes or until slightly risen and just firm to the touch. Serve immediately with a dollop of crème fraîche.

Serves 4

Serves 2

Microwave Chocolate Pudding

Preparation Time
10 minutes
Cooking Time
about 1 minute 10 seconds

- ◆ 2½ tbsp cocoa powder
- ◆ 2 tbsp golden syrup
- ◆ 6 tbsp self-raising flour
- ◆ 2½ tbsp caster sugar
- ◆ 1 medium egg
- ◆ 1½ tbsp mild oil
- ◆ 1½ tbsp milk
- ◆ 40g (1½ oz) white chocolate, finely chopped
- ◆ cream or ice cream to serve (optional)

**NUTRITIONAL
INFORMATION**
Per Serving (without cream/
ice cream) 640 calories, 21g fat
(of which 7g saturates), 106g
carbohydrate, 0.6g salt

1 Divide 1 tbsp cocoa powder equally between two standard mugs. Add 1 tbsp golden syrup to each and mix to a paste. Measure the flour, caster sugar and remaining 1½ tbsp cocoa powder into a medium bowl. Crack in the egg, and add the oil and milk. Mix well, then stir in the white chocolate.

2 Divide the mixture equally and tidily between the mugs, then microwave on full power (800W) for 1 min 10 seconds. Serve in the mugs, or turn on to a plate, adding cream or ice cream, if you like.

Romantic Rose Chocolates

Preparation Time
10 minutes, plus freezing
Cooking Time
about 1 minute

- 50g (2oz) white chocolate, chopped
- 50g (2oz) milk chocolate, chopped
- 50g (2oz) plain chocolate, chopped
- a selection of sprinkles, coloured sugar, gold leaf and sugar roses to decorate

NUTRITIONAL INFORMATION
Per chocolate **22 calories, 1.2g fat (of which 0.7g saturates), 3g carbohydrate, 0g salt**

1 Put each type of chocolate into a small, microwave-safe bowl. Put the bowls side by side in the microwave and heat on full power for 1 minute. Continue heating for 10 second bursts until the chocolates are melted and smooth (you may need to take them out at different times).

2 Meanwhile, line two baking sheets with baking parchment. Drop scant teaspoonfuls of the different types of melted chocolate on to the prepared sheets, spacing a little apart, then smooth into rounds with the back of a teaspoon.

3 Decorate the chocolates with sprinkles, coloured sugar, gold leaf or sugar roses. Freeze for 10 minutes to set, then pack into a tissue-lined box and give with love.

Makes about 36

Makes 16

Fancy Chocolate Biscuits for Friends and Family

Preparation Time
15 minutes, plus chilling
Cooking Time
about 15 minutes

- 375g pack ready rolled puff pastry
- 5 tbsp chocolate hazelnut spread
- 1½ tbsp chopped and ready roasted hazelnuts
- 1 egg, beaten

NUTRITIONAL INFORMATION
Per Serving 149 calories,
9g fat (of which 5g saturates),
15g carbohydrate, 0.2g salt

1 Unroll the puff pastry on a lightly floured work surface and spread over the chocolate hazelnut spread right to the edges of the pastry. Sprinkle over the chopped hazelnuts. Starting from one of the shorter sides, roll the pastry up to the middle, then roll the pastry up from the other short edge to the middle.

2 Transfer the roll to a baking sheet and brush with the beaten egg. Chill in the refrigerator until firm.

3 Preheat the oven to 220°C (200°C fan) mark 7. Using a serrated knife, cut the chilled roll into 16 slices, about 1cm (½in) thick.

4 Put the biscuit slices flat on two baking sheets, making sure that they are spaced well apart as they will puff up during cooking, and bake for about 15 minutes until golden. Using a spatula, transfer the slices to a wire rack to cool – if you can resist them!

Optional Glaze
Mix 40g (1½oz) icing sugar and enough orange juice or water to make a paste (about ½–¾ tbsp) together in a small bowl. Drizzle over the cooled biscuits and serve.

Summer Berry Cakes

Preparation Time
10 minutes
Cooking Time
12–15 minutes

- ◆ 400g (14oz) mixed summer berries, such as strawberries, raspberries, blueberries, blackberries and redcurrants
- ◆ 1 large egg
- ◆ 15g (½oz) caster sugar
- ◆ 40ml (1½fl oz) skimmed milk
- ◆ 1 tsp vanilla extract
- ◆ 25g (1oz) plain flour, sifted
- ◆ ½ tsp baking powder
- ◆ icing sugar to dust

NUTRITIONAL INFORMATION
Per Serving 99 calories,
2g fat (of which 0.5g saturates),
17g carbohydrate, 0.2g salt

1 Preheat the oven to 200°C (180°C fan) mark 6 and put a baking sheet on the middle shelf to heat up. Thickly slice any large strawberries, then divide the fruit among four 200ml (7fl oz) individual shallow ovenproof dishes.

2 Put the egg and caster sugar into a medium bowl and, using hand-held electric beaters, beat for about 3 minutes until the mixture is pale and fluffy. Next, quickly beat in the milk and vanilla, followed by the flour and baking powder.

3 Spoon the cake mixture over the berries in the dishes and put into the oven on the baking sheet. Bake for 12–15 minutes until the cake is cooked through and golden. Dust with icing sugar and serve immediately.

Cook's Tip
A large ovenproof serving dish will work just as well as individual dishes – it should be big enough so the berries lie no more than two deep. Extend the cooking time to 15–20 minutes.

Serves 4

Makes about 20 cookies

Tea Break Cookies

Preparation Time
10 minutes
Cooking Time
12–15 minutes, plus cooling

- ◆ 125g (4oz) unsalted butter, softened, plus extra to grease
- ◆ 100g (3½oz) soft light brown sugar
- ◆ 50g (2oz) golden syrup
- ◆ 140g (4½oz) plain flour
- ◆ 1 medium egg
- ◆ 100g (3½oz) jumbo oats
- ◆ 1 tsp ground cinnamon
- ◆ 75g (3oz) sultanas
- ◆ 75g (3oz) pecan halves, roughly chopped
- ◆ 40g (1½oz) plain chocolate, melted, to decorate

NUTRITIONAL INFORMATION
Per Cookie 167 calories,
9g fat (of which 4g saturates),
20g carbohydrate, 0g salt

1 Preheat the oven to 170°C (150°C fan) mark 3. Lightly grease two large baking sheets.

2 Mix the butter, sugar, syrup, flour, egg, oats, cinnamon, sultanas and nuts together in a large bowl until well combined. Put large tablespoonfuls of the mixture on to the prepared baking sheets, spacing them well apart.

3 Bake for 12–15 minutes until golden. Leave to cool for 10 minutes on the baking sheet, then drizzle with melted chocolate. Serve immediately, or leave to set first. Store set cookies in an airtight container for up to three days.

Florentines

Preparation Time
5 minutes
Cooking Time
8–10 minutes, plus cooling

- 65g (2½oz) unsalted butter, plus extra to grease
- 50g (2oz) golden caster sugar
- 2 tbsp double cream
- 25g (1oz) sunflower seeds
- 20g (¾oz) chopped mixed candied peel
- 20g (¾oz) sultanas
- 25g (1oz) natural glacé cherries, roughly chopped
- 40g (1½oz) flaked almonds, lightly crushed
- 15g (½oz) plain flour
- 125g (4oz) plain chocolate (at least 70% cocoa solids), broken into pieces

NUTRITIONAL INFORMATION
Per Slice **115 calories,**
8g fat (of which 4g saturates),
11g carbohydrate, 0.1g salt

1 Preheat the oven to 180°C (160°C fan oven) mark 4. Lightly grease two large baking sheets. Melt the butter in a small, heavy-based pan. Add the sugar and heat gently until dissolved, then bring to the boil. Remove from the heat and stir in the cream, sunflower seeds, peel, sultanas, cherries, almonds and flour. Mix until evenly combined. Put heaped teaspoonfuls on to the baking sheets, spacing well apart to allow for spreading.

2 Bake one sheet at a time, for 6–8 minutes, until the biscuits have spread considerably and the edges are golden brown. Using a large, plain, metal biscuit cutter, push the edges into the centre to create neat rounds. Bake for a further 2 minutes or until deep golden. Leave on the baking sheet for 2 minutes, then transfer to a wire rack to cool completely.

3 Melt the chocolate in a heatproof bowl over a pan of gently simmering water, stirring occasionally. Spread on the underside of each Florentine and mark wavy lines with a fork. Put, chocolate side up, on a sheet of baking parchment until set.

Makes 18

Index

A

almonds, trout with 172–3
Amaretti with lemon mascarpone
    290–1
anchovy & courgette burgers 196–7
apple
    compôte 24–5
    mash 268
    slaw 224
apricot, baked, & almonds 292–3
artichoke 68–9, 112–13
    mint & seafood pasta 146–7
asparagus 176
    & duck egg dippers 57
    & steak stir-fry 247
aubergine 272–3
    & chickpea pilau 211

B

bacon 74, 96–7, 188–9
    BLT-topped bagels 17
    chilli & sage pasta 127
    & lentil pasta 128–9
    & sweetcorn chowder 39
bagels, BLT-topped 17
banana 20
    & Brazil nut smoothie 26–7
    & pecan muffins 23
    sticky banoffee pies 316
beans 98–9, 104–5, 132, 222
    black-eyed bean chilli 213
    black-eye, greens & chicken 237
    broad, & feta salad 90–1
    butter, & pesto cod 168–9
    chilli, cake 208–9
    flageolet, salad 114–15
    mixed, salad 270
    sprouted, & mango salad 103
    on toast 16
    veggie burgers 206–7
    white, salad 92–3

beef
    fruity stir-fry 246
    quick stroganoff 275
    sesame 276–7
    sesame skewers, & noodle salad
        278–9
    sweet chilli stir-fry 242–3
    see also steak
beetroot grated salad 86–7
berries
    & white choc crêpes 289
    summer cakes 326–7
    with toasted oats 11
    see also specific berries
biscuits
    fancy chocolate 324–5
    tea break cookies 328–9
black-eyed bean chilli 213
blini, jumbo salmon 75
blue cheese
    mushroom pappardelle & steak
        281
    spinach & pasta 134
blueberry 20, 308–9
    & lemon pancakes 22
Brazil nut & banana smoothie 26–7
bread
    orange eggy 21
broccoli 142–3, 242–3
    & goat's cheese soup 52–3
    & courgette shells 124–5
bruschetta
    breakfast 20
    halloumi & pepper 56
Brussels sprouts, chestnuts &
    shallots 79
bulgur wheat
    & salmon pilau 166
    with harissa lamb 248–9
burgers
    courgette & anchovy 196–7
    curried tofu 204–5
    veggie bean 206–7

C

cakes
    summer berry 326–7
    see also muffins
caramel warm puddings 318–19
carrot with mint & lemon 78
cheese 20, 70
    cheat's macaroni 142–3
    cheesy spinach muffins 13
    four-cheese gnocchi 135
    & ham with chicory 66
    see also specific cheeses
chestnuts, shallots & Brussels
    sprouts 79
chicken
    balsamic pasta 132
    basil & lemon 236
    black-eye beans & greens 237
    Caesar salad 106
    cheat's oven Kievs 235
    club sandwich 67
    easy Thai red curry 254–5
    fatijas 258–9
    garlic & thyme 260–1
    & ginger broth 49
    Jerk 228
    laksa 229
    Mediterranean 234
    Mexican, & pepper salsa 231
    quick coronation 80–1
    speedy pilaf 230
    spiced tikka kebabs 232–3
    stuffed breasts 256–7
    Thai green curry 252–3
chickpea 89, 220–1
    & aubergine pilau 211
chicory, ham & cheese 66
chilli, black-eyed bean 213
chilli dressing, warm 244–5
chips, fish & 194–5
chocolate
    cheat's soufflés 312–13
    cheat's tiramisu 300–1
    -dipped strawberries 317
    fancy biscuits 324–5

florentines 330–1
luscious pots 302–3
microwave pudding 320–1
quick gooey puddings 294–5
romantic rose chocolates 322–3
torte 298–9
warm caramel puddings 318–19
see also white chocolate
chorizo
   & melon salad 111
   pea & Parmesan soup 38
   tomatoes & cod 167
Christmas pud, quick 310–11
cinnamon pancakes 297
cod
   & crusted minted pea mash 170–1
   chorizo & tomatoes 167
   pesto, & butter beans 168–9
compôte, apple 24–5
cookies, tea break 328–9
   Florentines 330–1
courgette 89, 92–3, 110
   & anchovy burgers 196–7
   & broccoli shells 124–5
   & fennel pasta 130–1
   & goat's cheese spaghetti 144–5
   & ribbon pasta 120–1
couscous
   -stuffed mushrooms 64
   fruit, & curry pork steak 220–1
   & smoked fish salad 107
   spicy, & lamb 272–3
crab
   classic dressed 182–3
   crispy cakes 184
   quick cakes 184
   simple salad 102
crêpes, white choc & berry 289
cucumber & warm smoked salmon
   salad 100
curry
   curried tofu burgers 204–5
   easy red Thai 254–5
   our favourite 155
   pheasant 284–5
   pork steak 220–1
   satay pork 226–7
   Thai green 252–3
   Thai green prawn pasta 126
   Thai vegetable 212

tikka spiced kebabs 232–3

D

Dover sole, 174–5

E

egg 88, 98–9, 104–5, 175
   classic omelette 200
   creamy baked 14
   duck, & asparagus dippers 57
   French toast 18–19
   orange eggy bread 21
   & pepper pizza 207
   scrambled, & smoked salmon 15
   spinach & goat's cheese frittata
     201
Eton mess, boozy 308–9

F

fatijas, chicken 258–9
fennel
   & courgette pasta 130–1
   & sausage gnocchi 139
feta & broad bean salad 90–1
fig 96–7
   & Stilton salad 108–9
fish
   Cajun wraps 76–7
   & chips 194–5
   Dover sole 174–5
   fast soup 35
   goujons 192–3
   grilled, with rocket pesto 177
   simple smoked haddock 190–1
   smoked, & couscous salad 107
   trout with almonds 172–3
   zingy one-pan 176
   see also specific fish
fishcakes
   oriental prawn & squid 156
   salmon & pea 158–9
   spicy salmon, & zesty veg 157
florentines 330–1
French toast 18–19
frittata, spinach & goat's cheese 201

G

gammon
   cumin-spiced 223
   ham & pea soup 50–1
   with pineapple salsa 264
gnocchi
   bake 136–7
   easy four-cheese 135
   fennel & sausage 139
   pesto 138
goat's cheese 256–7
   & broccoli soup 52–3
   & spinach frittata 201
   & walnut salad 84–5
   & courgette spaghetti 144–5
goujons, fish 192–3
gratin, mango, & sabayon 296

H

haddock
   simple smoked haddock 190–1
   smoked, kedgeree 175
hake
   fish & chips 194–5
   fish goujons 192–3
halloumi & pepper bruschetta 56
ham
   cheese & chicory 66
   & pea soup 50–1
harissa lamb 248–9
herb
   & polenta crusted plaice 180
   lamb cutlets 269
   & lemon soup 42–3
   sauce 165
   sausages, & mustard dip 266–7
honey sauce, fiery 238–9

K

kebabs, spiced tikka 232–3
kedgeree, smoked haddock 175

L

laksa, chicken 229

lamb
  chops, & crispy garlic potatoes 271
  crisp crumbed cutlets 274
  harissa, & bulgur wheat 248–9
  herb cutlets 269
  & spicy couscous 272–3
  spring, & flageolet bean salad 114–15
  steaks, & mixed bean salad 270
leeks, pasta with pancetta & mushrooms 149
lemon
  & blueberry pancakes 22
  & herb soup 42–3
  mascarpone, & Amaretti 290–1
  passion pots, luscious 36–7
lentil & bacon pasta 128–9

M

macaroni cheese, cheat's 142–3
mackerel, smoked
  & orange salad 110
Madeira sauce 280
mango 246
  & sprouted bean salad 103
  gratin, with sabayon 296
melon & chorizo salad 111
meringue 308–9
  raspberry pie 304–5
miso & pork noodle soup 44–5
mozzarella
  Parma ham & rocket pizza 262–3
  & peach salad 94–5
muesli, energy-boosting 12
muffins
  banana & pecan 23
  cheesy spinach 13
mushroom
  & blue cheese pappardelle, with steak 281
  couscous-stuffed 64
  linguine 148
  pasta with leeks & pancetta 149
mussel
  creamy chowder 36–7
  & potato stew 188–9
mustard dip 266–7

N

nectarine in spiced honey & lemon 288
noodles
  easy 210
  Japanese pork with vermicelli 140–1
  pork stir-fry with chilli & mango 216–17
  salad 278–9
  soup, pork & miso 44–5
  soup, Vietnamese turkey 46–7
  spiced-up salmon 160–1
  warm smoked salmon & cucumber salad 100
nuts
  spicy 73
  see also specific nuts

O

oats
  energy-boosting muesli 12
  porridge with dried fruit 10
  tea break cookies 328–9
  toasted, with berries 11
olive 68–9, 120–1
omelette, classic 200
orange
  eggy bread 21
  & smoked mackerel salad 110

P

pancakes
  cinnamon 297
  lemon & blueberry 22
pancetta, spaghetti alla Carbonara 118–19
  pasta with leeks, pancetta & mushrooms 149
Parma ham 88, 94–5, 108–9, 274
  rocket & mozzarella pizza 262–3
  sage & pork steaks 265
Parmesan, chorizo & pea soup 38
parsnip & Stilton soup 30–1
passion fruit & lemon pot 36–7
pasta

bacon, chilli & sage 127
balsamic chicken 132
blue cheese & spinach 134
broccoli & courgette shells 124–5
cheat's macaroni cheese 142–3
chilli squid linguine 122–3
courgette & fennel 130–1
hot-smoked salmon & mascarpone 162–3
leeks, pancetta & mushrooms 149
lentil & bacon 128–9
mushroom linguine 148
pea & tortellini chunky soup 48
pesto 60–1
ribbon, & courgettes 120–1
seafood, artichoke & mint 146–7
spring onion, pea & mint penne 133
steak, blue cheese & mushroom pappardelle 281
Thai green prawn curry 126
see also spaghetti
pea 166
  & ham soup 50–1
  mint & spring onion penne 133
  minted mash, cod crusted with 170–1
  Parmesan & chorizo soup 38
  & salmon fishcakes 158–9
  & tortellini chunky soup 48
peach & mozzarella salad 94–5
pecan & banana muffins 23
pepper 103, 234, 242–3, 246, 258–9
  & egg pizza 207
  & halloumi bruschetta 56
  red, & tomato, roasted, soup 34
  salsa 231
  & tuna salad 98–9
  zesty 157
pesto
  cod, & butter beans 168–9
  gnocchi 138
  pasta 60–1
  rocket 177
pheasant curry 284–5
pies
  sticky banoffee 316
  raspberry meringue 304–5
pilaf, speedy chicken 230
pilau

aubergine & chickpea 211
salmon & bulgur wheat 166
pineapple 218–19
&prawn skewers 65
salsa 264
pizza
bread 68–9
egg & pepper 207
mozzarella, Parma ham & rocket
262–3
plaice with herb & polenta crust 180
poppadom scoops 72
pork
chilli & mango stir-fry 222
chops, & apple mash 268
curry steak, & fruit couscous
220–1
escalopes, & apple slaw 224
flash in the pan 222
hot & sour soup 40–1
Japanese, with vermicelli 140–1
& miso noodle soup 44–5
satay curry 226–7
steaks, sage & Parma ham 265
sweet & sour stir-fry 218–19
porridge, with dried fruit 10
potato 98–9, 104–5, 167, 222, 244–5
apple mash 268
chips 194–5
crispy garlic 271
& mussel stew 188–9
prawn
chilli king 154
king, Thai-style salad 101
our favourite curry 155
party 74
& pineapple skewers 65
smoky cocktail 54–5
special fried rice 152–3
& squid fishcakes 156
Thai green curry 252–3
Thai green curry pasta 126
pumpkin spiced soup 32–3

R

rarebit, Welsh 70
raspberry meringue pie 304–5
rice

coriander 181
smoked haddock kedgeree 175
special prawn fried 152–3
see also pilaf; pilau
rocket
mozzarella & Parma ham pizza
262–3
pesto 177

S

sabayon & mango gratin 296
salad
broad bean & feta 90–1
chicken Caesar 106
couscous & smoked fish 107
eggs Florentine 88
goat's cheese & walnut 84–5
grated beetroot 86–7
hot-smoked salmon 104–5
Italian-style steak 112–13
king prawn Thai-style 101
Mediterranean 89
melon & chorizo 111
mixed bean 270
mozzarella & peach 94–5
noodle 278–9
orange & smoked mackerel 110
Provençale tuna & pepper 98–9
simple crab 102
simple winter 96–7
spring lamb & flageolet bean
114–15
sprouted bean & mango 103
steak, & warm chilli dressing
244–5
Stilton & fig 108–9
warm smoked salmon &
cucumber 100
white bean 92–3
salmon
& bulgur wheat pilau 166
cracker-crusted 164
hot-smoked, & mascarpone pasta
162–3
hot-smoked, salad 104–5
jumbo blini 75
& pea fishcakes 158–9
poached, & herb sauce 165

smoked, & scrambled eggs 15
smoked, Mediterranean salad 89
smoked, warm, & cucumber salad
100
spiced-up noodles 160–1
spicy fishcakes 157
salsa
pepper 231
pineapple 264
sandwiches, chicken club 67
satay pork curry 226–7
sausage
& fennel gnocchi 139
herb, & mustard dip 266–7
Italian stew 225
scallop with ginger 186–7
seafood, artichoke & mint pasta
146–7
shallot, chestnut & Brussels sprouts
79
skewers
prawn & pineapple 65
sesame beef 278–9
slaw, apple 224
smoothie, Brazil nut & banana 26–7
sorbet, tutti frutti 314–15
soufflés, cheat's choc 312–13
soup
broccoli & goat's cheese 52–3
chunky pea & tortellini 48
creamy mussel chowder 36–7
fast fish 35
healing chicken & ginger broth 49
herb & lemon 42–3
hot & sour pork 40–1
parsnip & Stilton 30–1
pea, Parmesan & chorizo 38
pea & ham 50–1
pork & miso noodle 44–5
roasted red pepper & tomato 34
spiced pumpkin 32–3
sweetcorn & bacon chowder 39
Vietnamese turkey noodle 46–7
spaghetti
alla Carbonara 118–19
courgette & goat's cheese 144–5
spinach 88, 166, 168–9, 211, 230, 281
& goat's cheese frittata 201
blue cheese & pasta 134
cheesy muffins 13

spring greens, black-eye beans &
    chicken 237
spring onion
    pea & mint penne 133
squid
    chilli linguine 122–3
    & prawn oriental fishcakes 156
steak
    & asparagus stir-fry 247
    au poivre 282–3
    with blue cheese & mushroom
        pappardelle 281
    fillet, & Madeira sauce 280
    Italian-style salad 112–13
    salad, & warm chilli dressing
        244–5
stew
    Italian sausage 225
    mussel & potato 188–9
Stilton
    & fig salad 108–9
    & parsnip soup 30–1
stir-fries
    fruity beef 246
    pork, with chilli & mango 222
    steak & asparagus 247

sweet chilli beef 242–3
sweet chilli tofu 202
sweet & sour pork 218–19
strawberries, chocolate-dipped 317
sweetcorn & bacon chowder 39

T

tartlets, roasted veg 62–3
Thai
    -style salad, king prawn 101
    easy red curry 254–5
    green curry prawn pasta 126
    Thai green 252–3
    vegetable curry 212
tiramisu, cheat's 300–1
toast
    beans on 16
    French 18–19
tofu
    curried burgers 204–5
    marinated 203
    sweet chilli stir-fry 202
tomato
    cod & chorizo 167
    & red pepper, roasted, soup 34

thyme 71
torte, chocolate 298–9
trout, Mediterranean 178–9
    with almonds 172–3
tuna
    & coriander rice 181
    & pepper Provençale salad 98–9
turkey
    breast, & fiery honey sauce 238–9
    Vietnamese noodle soup 46–7
    zesty one-pan 240–1
tutti frutti sorbet 314–15

V

vegetable curry, Thai 212
vegetable tartlets 62–3
vegetables, zesty 157
veggie bean burgers 206–7

W

walnut & goat's cheese salad 84–5
Welsh rarebit 70
white chocolate 322–3
    & berry crêpes 289